For Christian —

I love you!

Yours,

[signature]

DRIVING IN LA

BRENDA BAKKE

Copyright © 2016 Brenda Bakke & Brenda Jean Bakke, Inc.

All rights reserved. No part of this book may be reproduced, stored, or transmitted by any means—whether auditory, graphic, mechanical, or electronic—without written permission of both publisher and author, except in the case of brief excerpts used in critical articles and reviews. Unauthorized reproduction of any part of this work is illegal and is punishable by law.

ISBN: 978-1-4834-5458-0 (sc)
ISBN: 978-1-4834-5459-7 (e)

Because of the dynamic nature of the Internet, any web addresses or links contained in this book may have changed since publication and may no longer be valid. The views expressed in this work are solely those of the author and do not necessarily reflect the views of the publisher, and the publisher hereby disclaims any responsibility for them.

Any people depicted in stock imagery provided by Thinkstock are models, and such images are being used for illustrative purposes only. Certain stock imagery © Thinkstock.

Lulu Publishing Services rev. date: 07/01/2016

For Jenny

Contents

1 - Oregon 1
2 - Umbrellas 6
3 - Rapes 8
4 - The Bus 15
5 - Fear 18
6 - Westwood 23
7 - My First Car 27
8 - Pasadena 30
9 - Trust 34
10 - The Trip 37
11 - Cocaine 41
12 - Venice 45
13 - Buck 49
14 - The Gift 53
15 - Favors 59
16 - Heart Seizure 61
17 - Prostitution 64
18 - Meeting the Man 68
19 - Independence 73
20 - Busted 80
21 - The Paper 86
22 - Hotel Room 89

Author's Note 97
About the Author 99

CHAPTER 1

OREGON

People don't want to allow me to be dark. That's why I hide from them now. Of course, I do run into them now and then, and they keep trying to help me. They keep telling me that I should be happy. And I think, well maybe, but there's all of these other things I need to think about. You know, like rapes, the story in my head about preschool, prostitution, or the ever-recurring infant nightmare of the moth, and I think, well how am I supposed to be happy all of the time when I've got all of this other stuff to think about.

You know, like jumping out of cars I'm riding in with some guy, sitting shotgun, smoking a cigarette, and drinking coffee in a to-go cup, while we're going really fast on the freeway, so I'd be sure to die, because I'd be so mangled by all of the other cars on the freeway that my body would just bounce all over the place. I mean, you'd hardly be able to even recognize me, or even be able to figure out who the hell I was, if it wasn't for the goddam guy driving the car, or maybe my dental records.

There's a lot of cars in LA. There's hardly any time of day now when there aren't a lot of cars. I remember when I first moved here, there weren't half as many cars as there are now.

You know what's so funny? I didn't even know how to drive when I first moved here. I swear to God. I took the bus everywhere for the first ten goddam months I was here. But, I was good at it. I'd taken the bus for the past five years in Oregon, so it wasn't such a big deal, because I was used to it. I used to go everywhere on the bus in Oregon, when I wasn't walking. You do a lot of walking in Oregon. Well, at least I did anyway.

And I was always very busy in those days, because I had a career in mind, a career ahead of me, so I worked really hard and moved as fast as I could. Even if I was riding on the bus, the slowest transportation on earth, other than the *mule* for crissakes, at least I was moving. But what I finally figured out was that I just had to get the hell out of there. I was just sick of the whole thing.

I was sick of the down vests, and the down parkas, and the Oregon Ducks, and being from Beaverton, and everyone wearing tennis shoes all the time. And even though one of the biggest tennis shoe manufacturing companies did originate right there in Beaverton, it just didn't seem natural that everyone had to wear them every single day of their lives. It just didn't seem right.

And the people who lived there, it seemed to me anyway, just had no ideas. They just didn't want to go anywhere. And this was an anomaly to me. I just wanted to live and grow and travel, and it seemed to me that all of these people just wanted to thrive on the quality of their barbeques and their lawn mowers, and that they would just be perfectly happy to have a heart seizure in their stupid tennis shoes while turning a couple of salmon steaks on the grill in front of the kids. I mean, what is that, and how is that anyway to live, you know?

I really didn't know how to drive when I first moved here. Although, back in Oregon when I was a kid around ten or something, my dad used to let me drive every once in a while. But it was this big truck with a camper on the back, so it wasn't even fun. He'd owned it for years, and it was big and old and ugly, and very large.

But anyway, about the driving thing. We'd be going along these forest highways in Oregon, from some camping trip, or from skiing, and he'd let me 'take over the wheel.' And his breath always smelled like coffee, and he always had a thermos of it in his truck. So when he talked to me, or gave me instructions, I couldn't even concentrate because of his horrible coffee breath. And he always made me drive so slow, at least twenty miles an hour under the speed limit, so how could I ever really learn how to drive?

I ran away from home when I was thirteen. Well, away from my mom and sister, anyway. It did take a few times to get the court to believe I was serious about it, so I just kept leaving, and would take the bus to go stay with some friends of my new stepmom. And the best thing about this couple I stayed with was that the husband was really good at ping pong, and he taught me how to play really well.

But the first time I decided to run away was the worst. My mom was home, and I had to shove her away from the front door to get out, and it was all tearful and yelling, so it was pretty awful. But after that, I would leave when she wasn't around. I mean, I felt pretty terrible about all the shoving and yelling and stuff, and I just didn't want to have to go through it again.

Anyway, I was finally away from my mom, and could just be with my dad. But the whole thing wasn't as fun as I thought it was going to be, and I was nervous around him all the time, because I really didn't know him. Of course, I knew he was a workaholic and all, but I always thought that I could help him be happier and to get more out of life than just working all of the time. In fact, I really thought that my new stepfamily would help. I even thought that they already had, and that's why I went there.

And before I left her, my mom wouldn't even let me be around him at all, so how could I even know what it was like to stay with him for an extended period of time or anything?

And once I was actually living with him, I found out that my mom was right about what it was like to be around him 24-7. Like, there was this one time he left us all in this restaurant because he had to take off on some assignment. I mean, we sat there for hours just waiting for him to come back, but eventually we ordered dinner and took a taxi home. Or he'd fall asleep in his office that was right next to my bedroom, not because he wanted to be near me, but because his best friend IBM's cursor was still blinking at the last sentence he'd left off on.

Now, the stepfamily was pretty great. My stepmom used to make the best whole wheat bread from scratch, and we'd diet and drink smoothies for breakfast, and my step sister taught me how to play tennis really well. But we really didn't belong together. Especially after all the drama and all. We went through a lot of drama. In fact, one time to get dad to stop ignoring us, we faked this whole suicide thing. And my stepmom promised me a new hat if we pulled it off. I was crazy about hats in those days.

So when he got home, I had to cry and freak out while I told him about this whole suicide attempt she'd made by trying to drown herself in the pool. We splashed a lot of water around the edges of the pool, and she was in bed, *supposedly* recovering. And it did have the required effect, because he actually did stop ignoring us for a week or so. Then he was gone for another week, and came home one night saying he was sorry, but he just had deadlines to get out and that he was sorry he didn't call to let us know where he was.

But I guess the best thing about that whole thing is that I got my new hat.

Anyway, the worst thing is that I never believed that I would be so uncomfortable around him once I became a ward of the court, and could live wherever I wanted. I had tried so hard to be away from my mom, that I thought everything would be so normal once I'd finally gotten away from her and my sister. But, as I said before, it wasn't like that at all.

He made me drive so goddam slow all the time, so when I drove, he drove me nuts saying I was going too fast or to slow down, or that a 'defensive driver is a good driver.' I mean, what does that mean?

And the worst thing about his stupid truck-and-camper thing was that he would come to my junior high tennis matches, and pretend to watch me play tennis while he sat in the camper working. Now, how in the world is anyone supposed to concentrate on their tennis match when everyone in the whole goddam world knows your dad is sitting in a stupid camper out on the street, scribbling away like mad on some legal pad, and not even watching. I mean, even if everyone didn't know he was there, I did.

And just how was that supposed to make me play tennis any better, you know? But, I suppose it was pretty nice that he showed up at all.

CHAPTER 2

UMBRELLAS

I stole a car when I was fourteen. It was very interesting. It was on one of those real rainy Oregon days. Not that you would know the difference between a *real* rainy Oregon day, or just a *rainy* Oregon day, but I suppose it doesn't really matter.

Anyway, the rain was just pouring straight down, a *real* rainy Oregon day, and I'd just been on some stupid modeling interview that I'd gotten a ride to, so I was all dressed up, and wearing high heels, and carrying this ridiculously huge portfolio holder that only had about four stupid photos in it, and of course I had no goddam umbrella. I never had. The whole time growing up in Oregon, I had never possessed an umbrella, or at least one that I am aware of. In fact, I still don't.

Actually, I did have one once, a few years ago, that I kept in my car for the very occasional California Emergency Rainy Day, but I gave it away to this homeless guy in Santa Barbara that I felt sorry for. I mean, the rain was pretty much as bad as it gets in California, and there he was, looking so lost and wet, so of course I had to give it to him.

Anyway, about the umbrella thing. Doesn't that seem weird? I grew up walking to school every day in Oregon, and I never used an umbrella. But, of course, I did wear a lot of plastic and rubber. Well, I suppose you'd have to be from Oregon to understand all that.

So, I'd been walking in the rain in what I eventually discovered was a very large circle, trying to find the goddam bus stop, and there I was, forty-five minutes worth of wandering around later in my high heels, back to where I'd started from.

But the best thing was that at that particular spot where I had stopped, there was this big parking lot with all these cars parked in it and the very first car I looked into had the keys in it. I swear to God, *the very first car.* So, I got in. I don't remember what color it was, but I do remember that it was one of those Japanese cars, and that meant that there were certain gears I needed to understand. But, I didn't. It took me at least ten minutes just to get out of the stupid parking lot. I don't know how I did it, but I did.

Of course, I did get stuck on a small slope for a few minutes, stalling over and over, and all of these cars honking behind me, but I finally got it into the right gear, and made it into the general vicinity of my neighborhood. And when I got to this cul de sac, about three blocks from my house, I got out of the car and started walking away, really fast.

Now that I think of it, the worst part was that I didn't know about the emergency brake thing, and while I was rounding the corner, peripherally, I noticed the car starting to roll *very slowly* down the street. But, I didn't stop to look back. I didn't do a goddam thing about it. I just kept going.

That was the worst part.

CHAPTER 3

RAPES

I've been raped twice. Well, three times really. I mean if you count it and all.

Now, of course you might think that I can just say that so easily, but you know what? Once you've lived a few years beyond the times you were raped, you kind of get over it. Especially if you don't tell anyone for a few years. Because, I think that if you told someone right away, right after it had just happened, like the next day, or within the next hour, you would be all obsessed with it and you could never just let it go, you know, just chalk it up for experience. And that's what I'm doing right now, just looking at it like it was a gift from God.

I mean, if I wasn't around to experience it, then it would've happened to someone else who might've told everyone in the whole goddam world, and they would've never gotten over it, you know what I mean? And if I would have ever reported it, the whole thing would be down on someone's forms, down on paper, and I would know exactly when it happened, and probably would have never been able to think about it in a Godlike way.

One of the first things that happened to me when I got to LA is that I got a ticket for hitchhiking off the curb. I mean, how stupid is that? Is there supposed to be some kind of manual of hitchhiker rules, or what?

I had just moved here on a train, so how am I supposed to know all the *rules* for crissakes.

So, I'm walking along Washington Boulevard in Playa Del Rey, which is where I first lived because I was staying with this bartender guy from Portland that I'd worked with in a restaurant called Reuben's, where I'd actually been a cook, and had to wear one of those tall white chef's hats and white coats with the big buttons, while I furiously ran around a kitchen cooking steaks and lobsters. It was a pretty classy place, and I really liked learning to cook like that. And he'd said before he quit to move to California that I could stay with him if I ever moved down, so I took him up on it. Of course I had no idea that it meant I would have to sleep on the floor of a crummy studio apartment that smelled like cat piss, but I wasn't feeling real particular at the time when I arrived on the train. And he picked me up from the train station and all. He really was a pretty nice guy.

Anyway, I thought I'd try to get a ride, instead of paying for the bus, to the Fox Hills Mall to apply for jobs, mainly because I was pretty broke at the time. Malls were a pretty big deal back in the 80s, especially in Beaverton. I mean, back then it was *the* place to go. The other stupid thing is that I knew practically nothing about curbs because they hardly exist in Beaverton. That's another thing you'd only know if you lived there.

So the police gave me the ticket, and I was real pissy with them, and told them that in the future I would make real sure that I kept my feet on the goddam curb whenever I was hitchhiking. I don't think they appreciated my swearing at all. And, the funny thing is that I never hitchhiked again. And I haven't to this day.

I finally got a ride to the mall, and actually landed a job at this men's Western Wear clothing store that also sold a lot of Cowboy hats. Now, the most interesting thing about that job was that I was trained in the art of 'hat-shaping', which is a skill most people would not be able to claim they share with me. I had to either stretch these hats to fit people's heads, or fashion the brims to the shape they wanted. This was done with a steamer, and shaping the brims was an art. I can tell you that, because it was usually some kind of Cowboy that came into this store, trying to shape their hats to impress their stupid Cowgirl girlfriends, and they were real particular about how their hat shape should be. It was a pretty boring job.

The first time I was raped was when I was seventeen, and still living in Oregon. I was living in this apartment complex with my two friends Nikki and Sara. I'd decided to move away from the stepfamily, after dad and my stepmom said they were getting a divorce, and dad just disappeared completely. It just didn't feel right to stay with them anymore. I mean, they weren't my real family or anything, and I felt pretty good about taking care of myself. So I just left.

The apartment was in this big complex, you know, the tri-level kind, with lots of stairways and separate buildings, a couple of pools, and a rec-room with a pool table and a couple of ugly fake-wood sofas with cushions covered in that ugly multi-colored upholstery.

Now, that's something I really hate, ugly upholstery. If you're going to design a durable fabric, why not at least make it halfway attractive, or at least even beautiful, you know? I remember being really upset about life once, and walking down the aisle of an airplane, and waiting for people to stuff their luggage into the overhead bins and commenting to a complete stranger next to me about how ugly everyone's luggage was. I mean there's some really ugly luggage out there. We laughed really hard at the idea, but I don't think the people around us really enjoyed the fact that we were making fun of their taste in luggage upholstery.

One of the funniest things that happened while I lived in this complex was that my girlfriends and I took some acid. At first we all got really hungry, so we decided to walk down to the Plaid Pantry to get some Ho Hos and some Cheetos or something, and there were cops there and we were real careful not to act funny or anything, and of course walked home laughing hysterically at how well behaved we'd been in front of the cops. Then for some reason we ended up behind all the apartment buildings outside, and walking down the narrow walkway between the fence and the buildings and we all saw this little dot up ahead, and finally when we got up to the dot, it turned out to be a little boy, and we just laughed and laughed at how the dot was a little boy. I felt really bad the next day about laughing at the poor little boy, and him not knowing what the hell was wrong with us.

So, there was this neighbor of ours, a big black guy that was always walking by the apartment, who lived in this same big complex. I hate to even say that he was a black man, only because too many crimes are placed on black men, and it makes me feel bad that I would say such a thing. I suppose it doesn't even matter what color his skin was. I guess I'm just trying to describe him. And, as I said, he was big, and he seemed not to notice things around him, real quiet and ominous in a way. I'd even tried to say hi to him a couple of times, and he seemed to just ignore me.

But, now that I look back, I suppose he knew when I was home alone and all, because I don't think he would have ever come by if he knew other people were there. I remember I couldn't find a clean shirt when I heard the knock at the door, and that I thought it was a neighbor of mine from upstairs, whose name I can't even remember now, which is weird because he was always coming by right after I'd gotten home from school, and was always asking if he could borrow a cigarette. I mean, how do you borrow a cigarette for crissakes?

Anyway, it didn't turn out to be my upstairs neighbor. Right now I know I would have been real happy to see him. I know now that if it *had* been him, I would have bought him a whole goddam carton of cigarettes. Sometimes in life you really go back over things and think, why didn't it happen different and why didn't I do such and such? But, life's not like that. You can't go back. You can never go back.

So this man, whose name I don't even know to this day, pushes his way into the door as soon as I'd opened it, and I can't say the rest, only that he kept saying that if I ever told anyone that he would kill me. I can't say the whole thing, only because I feel that if I describe it, I might never recover, and that it might take over my mind. He hurt me really bad. He really hurt me. It was face into the carpet, not moving, wide eyed bad. I don't remember him leaving, or how long it took me to move from where I was staring into the carpet. I do remember that I cleaned myself the best I could, found a clean shirt, and got my things and went to work as usual, on the bus.

I think it's pretty amazing that I made it to work on time, but I suppose it doesn't really take all that long to rape someone. I mean, it's not like we were languishing afterwards in each other's arms and smoking a cigarette together for crissakes. I was really quiet at work that night, but I just prepped my shrimp and rice pilaf and cooked my steaks to order.

And I knew, instinctually, that I could never say a word because of the way he would pass outside my window, outside of my apartment and look up at me, even when my friends were there, just looking up at me. I was too afraid that he really would kill me. It was his face. There was just something about his face, or in his eyes. I don't know.

And the second time was completely different.

These guys just came out of the blue. I was just leaving from this boring actor party in Pasadena, walking to my Mustang in the rain. And of course, I still had no goddam umbrella. I was eighteen and a half. And there they were, pulling over to the side of the road, in what appeared to be a yellow Volkswagen bug. These two completely American white guys that seemed like your typical high school jock types, you know?

We all go to high school, and we all know about the different types, like the nerdy math and science type guys, or the popular cheerleader type girls. And even if you were a typical white American jock type, you would know that, right? In fact, you would probably even tell a woman that about yourself on a first date and all, trying to impress the hell out of her while you were describing what you were like in high school, even if you're a forty year old now, and think you've turned out to be the most sensitive guy in the world, all into Yoga or Buddhist Zenism or whatever, you would still describe your past as having been in that jock type of group, right? And, of course I think it's important that I describe these guys for what they were, the color of their skin and all. I guess it's important to *describe* them, because as I said before, most of the crimes in the United States are blamed on black guys, and I don't think that's fair at all.

I mean, to me they were just a couple of white guys without faces. I will never be able to picture their faces. It's just like my black neighbor, he doesn't have a face anymore either. I think that anyone who does you harm doesn't deserve a face. They should all just be a blur in your mind, and should never become such a power that you cannot erase them in a mental way. Just erase them completely.

Anyway, all I thought was that they were going to be asking for directions to the boring actor party I'd been to, when the guy in the shotgun seat says that I was looking pretty fine, and got out of the stupid Volkswagen bug.

"Oh, where's the party? That's what we're looking for." he said, just laughing like it was the funniest thing in the world. And I remember his friend saying for us to move away so he could park, and I was saying goodbye and I hoped they had a good time, even though I knew it was a pretty boring party, when the friend stayed walking with me to where his friend was parking, and then it was dark.

I remember how strong and big the first guy was, grabbing me, and holding onto my arms, and putting me into the back seat of the car, and his friend laughing and folding back the driver's seat so he could hold onto me in the back seat next to me. Their lights were off, so no one passing in their cars could see what was going on. The big guy raped me first, and then his friend, and then they left me on the side of the road. I remember I was crying for my mom, and that no one saw me while I laid there in the dirt. I was glad that no one saw me, because I was all wet and naked from the waist down. They had taken my skirt and underwear that they had ripped off of me with them. It was very funny to them.

People still ask me why I never reported it. I've always told them that it's only because I never saw the license plate, and that it was too dark to identify the two shitheads. But, that's not really true. I mean, if I ever saw those two guys again, I would know them. I just would.

CHAPTER 4

THE BUS

I'd only been living in LA for a few weeks, when I received the official acceptance letter to The American Academy of Dramatic Arts, this acting school in Pasadena that I'd applied to back in Oregon before I'd graduated from high school. I was pretty happy about that.

So, I left the guy in Playa del Rey to work a couple waitressing jobs in Westwood for the summer, to save for my tuition and other living expenses. And when it came time to move to Pasadena, I still had no car, and had to move there on the bus from Westwood. I just didn't have enough cash for a taxi which would have run well over 100 bucks, and I'd spent all my savings on tuition and a room in an old lady's house in Pasadena, and didn't really know anyone well enough to ask for their help. Now, if you've never lived in LA, you would not even remotely understand the distance I'm talking about, unless of course you looked at a map. Moving from Westwood to Pasadena took me 3 busses, and it took me 3 trips to move everything, even though I didn't have much, mainly because I had to carry everything from one bus to the other.

The night when I was taking my last load of stuff on the stupid bus it was about 10:00, and I got stuck way the hell downtown LA on Wilshire Boulevard because there were no more number *204s* or whatever that night going to Pasadena. And you can probably gather that that was not such a good thing, being stuck in the middle of a big abandoned city, with hardly any traffic, and a bunch of crazies looking at my stuff, and no places open, except for one of those divey Mexican bar-restaurants, where the signs weren't even in English.

So there I am on the street, staring at this neon sign with the last one of my bags, one of these three multi-sized, drab olive green heavy duty plastic luggage bags that my dad had given to me. He was the kind of person who never gave away anything until it had completely worn out. I'm pretty sure that came from being a Norwegian. Like the American flag speedo bathing suit he wore until you could completely see parts of his butt straight through the lycra fabric that had worn down to practically nothing, until we had to say "Dad, why don't you throw it away? We can see your butt." But he always said that everything was worth something, and that he had paid good money for it and he wasn't about to throw away a perfectly good piece of clothing that had a couple more good years in it.

That's the thing about Norwegians. I mean, they even use the blood from a pig to put in their pancakes, because they don't waste a goddam thing. They have some really disgusting foods, like their cheeses that smell like death, and their Lutefisk, which is fish in some kind of lye, and all kinds of really scary things. If you really think about it, have you ever even *seen* a Norwegian restaurant in your life? Unless of course you're in Norway, for crissakes.

There I was, with the last of my earthly belongings, contained in this ugly green bag, and had come to a place where I felt sure to be killed just because I was an American born woman with a real social security number. And at that moment I couldn't imagine what I would find, or how I would be treated.

When I first moved to Southern California, I was told by other white Californians that the Mexicans were the most dangerous of all the people in the city, and that I should never even bother to talk to them because of their always trying to take advantage of you, and so on. But, when I walked into this Mexican bar, I discovered an enormous secret for myself. I found, and still know to this day, that most people from Mexico, or from any other South American country, are some of the kindest, most family-oriented people in this world, at least from what I've experienced in my lifetime so far. And here I was, a person who had no friends. No one had ever helped me in any way, other than the Playa del Rey guy, so I was used to that. I never asked anyone for help. And the very first people I needed were the people who had seemed the scariest to me.

So, I walk into this bar-restaurant, and hear this very unfamiliar Spanish music playing in the background, and I was very afraid, and very upset. But these people who were sitting there at the bar, and the people who worked there immediately noticed my emotional state, and started talking to me. *In English.* They asked me questions about what had happened and why I was so upset. I sat there on this barstool, and the bartender brought me a glass of water and some napkins, and I told this whole group of strangers what had happened to me, and they immediately started to figure out how to help me.

I know that I was pretty young at that time, and perhaps this is why they felt compelled to help me, or why they understood and tried to make me feel at ease. I can pretty much imagine that some of them had been through some similar circumstances by moving to this country on their own. I don't think most people can understand how difficult it is to try and be invisible in a place not your own, and to try and hide from authorities in the midst of the movement of a city. I have to believe that this kind of undertaking is true bravery, like a trust in the will of God, and that anyone who faces this type of change will face fear, and forever know the illusion of ease. But then, when you find yourself there where you dreamed you'd be, you may never find what you were looking for in the first place, and wonder why the hell you changed your entire life to be in a place far away from what you thought of as home.

So, anyway, two of the guys. Two of the sweet fucking Mexican guys, man, they take me all the way to the little old lady's house, all the way to goddam Pasadena, and they drop me and my bag off. And I never saw those people or those two guys again. They all just helped me, and never asked for anything back.

That was a good day.

CHAPTER 5

FEAR

I can completely remember my first time driving on Sunset Boulevard. The western part anyway, not the seedy eastern part past Highland, for crissakes. That's the crack whore, dumpy portion of the Boulevard. I don't even want to talk about *that* portion. One of the coolest things about Sunset Boulevard is that it stretches really far, all the way from Downtown LA to the Pacific Palisades, where it ends right at Gladstone's on the beach, this really great fish restaurant where you have to watch out for seagulls trying to steal all of your food. I mean, they'll just swoop right down and take off with your little foil wrapped pad of butter if you're not careful.

It's a famous road. You should see the early photographs of it sometime. It was just a dirt road surrounded by orchards and farms, cows and pigs, and lots of orange trees, acres and acres of orange trees. It was beautiful. I've seen a lot of the photographs of what LA used to look like. I've been here a long time now, and I'm just interested. I mean, the whole thing, it just stretched right out, and was all free and wild, you know? The mountains just cascading right out into the goddam ocean. No wonder the Indians lived here. It was beautiful.

I think that most people must think that Sunset Boulevard is a very glamorous road to drive on, because of its name, and of course the movie that was named after it. But now I know that it's really just a winding road that a lot of people speed on, trying to pass all the slow drivers, and getting all pissed off when there's too much traffic, and don't really give a shit if Bel Air is on one side, or that there are a lot of mansions all around them, or movie stars, or that UCLA is right there in its midst.

I think it's a sad place, really because there are all of these people selling maps to Movie Stars' homes, just sitting out there in the sun, with their sunglasses on and a hat, just waving these flags around like they're the greatest things in the world. Or the double-decker tourist busses giving tours of all these stars' homes.

They really kill me, the tourist busses. During the first few years after I moved here, I would wave to all the people when we were stopped at a stoplight, pretending I was someone really famous and all, and everybody would wave back. I'd wear my sunglasses, and some really great lipstick, and I *was* in a cool red Mustang after all. I mean, they were all so goddam desperate just to see a famous person, so anyone who waved to them would get them all excited, and they'd start flashing their stupid Nikons or whatever, just getting all excited and talking together and probably saying things like "Hey honey, who's that? Do you think they're *famous?*" It's pretty sad, really.

And then there are all of these Mexican women, who are maids to all of these rich people's houses, and you see them everyday, just waiting at the bus stops, like the one outside the Beverly Hills Hotel, under these quaint little shelters and all, so how could anyone ever think it could be a glamorous place?

I was a housekeeper when I was twelve. It was for the mom of some guy in my grade school, and I can tell you it wasn't very fun, and of course I took the bus there. It was this big old mansion with too many rooms, and you could tell that practically no one went into the rooms I cleaned. It was mostly dusting and vacuuming, but the worst part was cleaning the floor boards and the window sills. You know, they get all dirty and dusty, and no one in their right minds would ever notice if they were dirty and dusty or not for crissakes. But I had to clean them all the same, and I guess it's pretty great that I learned about cleaning those things. I really notice a clean floor board. And she always made me lunch, a tuna fish sandwich or something, so that was pretty nice. At least it gave me some sympathy for the Mexican ladies at the bus stop, because I had been one of them. But of course my bus stops never had quaint little shelters from the stupid rain in Oregon.

The Boulevard's curves are meant to be driven, and it's a wonderful ride as long as there's not all these people goddam sightseeing for crissakes. I mean, how is anyone who lives here supposed to get anywhere on time? How can anyone maintain a sense of normal life when there are all of these tourists and tourist busses driving so slow just to get a glimpse of so and so? Of course, most people wouldn't understand this coming from normal towns and all, but when you live here and you're trying to get somewhere, it can drive you crazy. I have no wonder why there are freeway shootings now and then. It's probably the goddam tourists driving the real drivers who live here crazy.

I was in this convertible car with this very handsome young law student whose name I can't even remember now. Anyway, I still have a couple of photographs of him in my picture box. One of the best pictures I have of him is this one that was taken at the beach at sunset, that he actually gave to me, and he's walking over this sand dune, the sun behind him in the west, so he's all silhouetted, like some beautiful, romantic man out of an Anais Nin novel or something. He seems very placid in that photograph, and I suppose this is why I still like that picture of him so much, and why I've kept it for all these years. He was dark and tall, but I remember that I didn't feel very safe with him. I guess that was why I didn't stay with him. Well, I did stay the night and have sex with him, after meeting him at the beach and making a date with him, but I don't think he ever really liked me or anything, so I never became his girlfriend, although he did ask me for my phone number.

The thing is, I gave him the wrong number. I think I was afraid of being attached, and of someone trying to stand in the way of my career. I think basically that I was kind of afraid of men at that time in my life. The fear of men is called Arrhenphobia, but I don't think I really had that because I had sex with the handsome lawyer guy. There's some pretty funny fears out there though, like Chorophobia, which is the fear of dancing, and Aulophobia, which is the fear of flutes. I mean, how can you be afraid of *flutes* for crissakes? I also have the fear of a bad clam, because a bad clam can make you really sick, and then you don't want to eat clam chowder anymore, and that's not right. There's some really great clam chowder out there, especially at Gladstone's.

I know the black rapist guy scared me, so I think that when I left Oregon, I felt like I would be safe again. It's funny, you know? At that time, I thought I'd left the fear behind, like nothing bad would ever happen to me again, only to enter into a brand new world of new fears. And here I am, even now, knowing that fear prevails in my mind. But I also know now that I'm not alone in this, that we all feel this in one way or another. Especially after 9-11. I mean, that's the day that really got everyone going on fear. It's too bad really.

Now that I think about it, the fear, my very own personal fear I mean, probably traces back to my first social experience. And the stupid thing about it was that it all happened because we were late. My mom was late, so I was late. Maybe that's why I'm always on time now, or even early most of the time. I mean, I'm nothing more than four years old or so, for crisssakes, and my mom just drops me off at my first day of preschool. I was probably wearing some old sweater and skirt, raggedy hand me down type outfit that came from my older sister, and I was carrying my coloring book when she sped right out of there. I think she had to get to a job interview or something, so I can't really be mad at my mom.

I walked into the school, and all the other kids were already sitting there on the floor in a circle with a big Folgers coffee can full of crayons in the middle. And the weird thing was, I swear to God, no one even looked up at me. So I sat down and folded out my stupid coloring book, and went to reach for a blue or whatever, and straight across from me was this *big* girl, staring at me like she wanted to kill me. And then, she stood straight up and motioned for all the other kids to follow her. And they did. And I just sat there.

I don't remember a lot of what happened after, except that I know I stood outside by myself for the rest of the day. I just stood right next to the swing set. I do remember that it was hot, and that there were bees. But what I remember most of all is that all I ate for lunch was my corn. In fact, if I ever wrote my stupid autobiography, I'd probably call it 'All I Ate Was My Corn.'

Maybe it's just fear of rejection, and the feeling of not ever being able to fit in, and I will always know that I'm alone, just like the rest of us.

CHAPTER 6

WESTWOOD

While I was still living in Westwood, I met this sad little guy named Tim. I only say he was sad because he seemed a little lonely. I was working as a waitress at this restaurant called Alice's Restaurant, you know, like the song. It was a pretty great place to work, because they made this coffee with cinnamon in it, and I just thought that was the most amazing coffee I'd ever had. And it had this jukebox, and someone would always put on the 'New York New York' song by Frank Sinatra, and when that happened, all of the waiters and bartenders would line up and do the final kicks at the end. It was pretty fun, and all the customers seemed to enjoy it and all, even if it meant their coffee wasn't going to be refilled for a couple of minutes or so. Alice's isn't there anymore. In fact, a lot of restaurants where I used to work are closed now, or the names have changed. It's interesting to drive past these places from my past, and see the changes.

Anyway, I'm not sure why I thought he was so lonely. And he had this funny little twitch to his face when he talked, and he never even once tried to kiss me. I mean, to me that was pretty strange, you know? Most guys always wanted to at least kiss me, for crissakes. Or maybe he was just too shy, I don't know. And I knew I was fairly *attractive* at least. So far, I haven't said that about myself, but I was. I'm sure you understand that that's a difficult thing to say about yourself.

Tim and his brother, whose name I can't remember now, had been joking around with me while they sat at one of the tables in my station, and then Tim asked me if I ever wanted to go out with him sometime. At that time I was pretty open and all, always telling people that I'd moved here from Oregon, and that I was saving my money to go to acting school, and how I was all serious about my career. Some people really liked that about me, that I was so open. I'm not even half as open as I was then.

I was living with three other roommates in an actual Frank Lloyd Wright apartment building in downtown Westwood, right in the midst of Fraternity Row. It was this really cool circular apartment building, with fountains, and curved stairs leading up to all of these individual entrances to the separate apartments, and I thought I was the goddam Queen of Sheba living there. I mean, I had never lived in a place that was so unique, and I really thought it was a beautiful spot. I never really got to know my roommates either, two guys and a girl that I shared a room with. I mean, they were gone all of the time, and I was usually gone at work, or taking the bus down Wilshire Boulevard to the beach.

It was my sister who helped me find the place. She was in school at UCLA, and suggested I take a look for rooms for rent on the student boards, so I did. And the place was only a few blocks away from her, where she was renting a room in one of the fraternity houses for the summer. And it was real kind of her to make the suggestion and all, because we hadn't ever been friends.

We hadn't really spoken to each other much since I got the custody change. But now, here we both were, in sunny California, where we'd always dreamed of ending up, listening to all those goddam Beach Boys songs and feeling pretty inadequate as a bunch of pale Oregonians, and watching the Miss America pageants where Miss Oregon never even got close to winning because she was probably too pale to even *try* to look good in the swimsuit competition. Well, at least I've never seen a Miss

Oregon ever make it into the goddam finals, I mean not ever. Anyway, that's how I ended up living in Westwood, of all the places I could've ended up in LA.

So, I go out with this Tim guy, and he's so shy that it's almost painful. He pulls up, and the first thing he says to me is "Hey! Want to go cruise Sunset Boulevard?" He said it like it was the *coolest* thing on the whole goddam planet to do. I wanted to be honest and tell him that I'd already done that with the tall dark handsome lawyer guy, but his face was so excited and pathetic at the same time that I just couldn't disappoint him, you know? And he kind of resembled this stuffed animal a girlfriend had when I was a kid that she'd named Piggy, even though it was a teddy bear, so I just said "Yeah…that'd be *great!*"

So at the end of the drive, and after some pretty good Thai food and sake, and after listening to the same information given to me by the dark haired lawyer guy about the history of Sunset Boulevard, the evening finally came to an end, and Tim dropped me off back at the Westwood apartment, and like I said, he didn't even try to kiss me or anything. I mean, he was *nice* and all, but I was really uncomfortable with him, because he was so nervous and shy, and I didn't want to know him. I just didn't want to anymore. But now that I think about it, he really was a nice guy.

I just stood there in the street, watching the red rear lights of his car make their way to the end of the road, and finally turn the corner, leaving me in the dark. I was glad to see his car was gone. I really was. I mean, I was so happy I just felt like celebrating. I felt this kind of freedom, like there was no one I had to goddam listen to, and be polite to, and all that crap. I mean, I'm a nice person, but sometimes you just feel a little sick about all you have to put up with in this world, all the crap of trying to be so goddam nice all the time, you know?

I remember I moved away from the stairs that led up to my apartment building, and kind of stumbled down the street because I was a little drunk from all the sake, and then I was suddenly coming upon all of the Fraternity Row Friday night parties. And while I was looking up at the life of these places, I heard a voice call to me from a balcony to come up and join them. I went up the stairs and into the building, not knowing the way, through rooms and up more stairs, and down this hallway. I came to a door that opened, and there he was. He gestured with his head for me to come inside the room, and closed the door, and locked it. We introduced ourselves, and he kissed me, and we had sex for a while. And then I left. Without a word. Without any words whatsoever. And after that, I prayed for weeks that I would never see his face again in sunlight, and that he'd never see me again either. And I still can't remember his name.

I don't even know why, but I'm glad.

CHAPTER 7

MY FIRST CAR

One of the best things that happened while I was going to school in Pasadena was that I bought my first car. The only way I could afford to buy it was because I was lucky enough to have been given a government grant for sixteen hundred dollars, mainly because I was so poor in high school, but also from getting such good grades. It was really meant to help me pay for the Academy, but the bus was getting kind of old after ten months of being here.

It was a red 1965 Mustang, with a tan interior. I bought the car from a used car lot for exactly sixteen hundred dollars, and just drove away, without really even knowing how to drive. Of course, it was a hell of a lot easier than the car I'd stolen when I was fourteen, because it was an automatic. I just drove around, all of the Sunday afternoon when I'd bought it, and when night came, I remember just pulling over to the side of a wide road, near a street lamp. It was one of those really old Pasadena neighborhoods that was real quiet and safe, with lots of old trees, and big houses, and those tall antique street lamps. And in the darkness of night, not knowing where I was, I just got out and laid on my back on the warm hood of the car, my head against the windshield and stared at the moon.

You know, sometimes you just have to look at the moon all by yourself, and imagine how small you really are. You just have to imagine what's out there, and think about infinity, and all the things that you don't really know yet, or are just waiting to figure out the things you already knew. So that's what I did. I just laid there for the longest time, and thought about stuff, about how I was feeling pretty goddam lucky, owning my own car, and living in a pretty great room in Pasadena, with my own private claw foot bathtub, just following my dream.

When I woke up, still on the hood of my new car, I felt like it had only been an hour or so, but of course it really wasn't. Actually, it was already morning, and the birds were just chirping the hell out of the whole goddam neighborhood. And once I was really awake, I started to get really hungry. So I drove around looking for a 24 hour Burger King or something, but never did end up finding one that was open. But I did need gas. I had to be at school in a couple of hours, so I pulled up to this Texaco station or whatever it was, and didn't even know how to put gas in the car. I mean, I was really embarrassed, but I told the gas station guy that I was from Oregon and all, and that you can't just drive right up and pump your own gas in Oregon, and that I'd really appreciate it if he would help me.

And actually, he turned out to be a pretty nice gas station attendant because he showed me where the gas cap was, and how you could set the pump to let it automatically go off once the tank was full, and that it wasn't good to top it off, no matter what. Not that I knew what *top it off* meant, but I just said "Okay, I'll never do that." Then he showed me how to check my oil, and where all the various fluid gauges were. I mean, this guy was taking all the time in the world to show me this stuff, and I was going to be late for school, so I tried to hurry him along. But he seemed like he was at least a hundred years old for crissakes, and like I said he was a really nice gas station guy, so I listened real patient, and finally got the hell out of there.

Now that I think of it, he probably would've liked to have gotten some kind of tip or something, but I didn't know a lot about tipping people in those days. So now I feel really bad that I never went back to give him a nice tip, you know, to buy his wife some flowers or his grandkids some toys or something. I just never did it.

He's probably not even alive now, so there's really no point in thinking about it, but I do.

CHAPTER 8

PASADENA

A few weeks later, I was getting pretty good at driving. I'd even drive on the freeway in Pasadena for a couple of exits, just for practice. Of course, the merging thing was the scariest part of all, but eventually I got the hang of it. Plus, the best thing about my Mustang was that it had a 389 engine, so power and speed were never a problem. And then I figured it would probably be a smart thing to get a driver's license.

Getting it was pretty easy because here in LA practically anyone can pass the driver's test. And you'd understand that perfectly well if you lived here. I mean, people are always complaining about other drivers in LA. In fact, sometimes my sister will call me from her car phone, and we can hardly have a conversation without her talking about how bad the traffic is, or even swearing at other drivers while she's driving. Eventually I had to tell her not to call me anymore when she was driving. And of course everyone that complains about other drivers never think that they *ever* do anything wrong.

But once you've been to places like New York, or Mexico City, or especially Manila, I mean, you can't really complain. I guess you'd have to have been to all these places to appreciate what I'm saying, but they are all complete maniacs in those cities when they drive.

When I finally got my driver's license, I was almost nineteen. And the guy who gave me my driver's test was real serious and boring, so I felt kind of sorry for him. I could tell he needed to have a good time and all, because of the expression on his face, you know, like he wanted to die or something. And he was big and fat, and really sweaty the whole time, and his name was Boris. So I tried to make good old sweaty Boris laugh with some of my own personal insights about drivers I knew, while he kept wiping away at his big sweaty forehead with his big semi-white handkerchief. I kept saying things about how my dad drove so slow, and about how other drivers were probably saying, or actually screaming at him, to go faster, and yelling things like *God! What a jerk! Learn how to drive the speed limit grandpa!* But I never made him laugh, not even once.

The worst thing is that I say things like that all of the time now when I'm driving. I mean, most old people drive so slow. And I feel sorry for them and all, because they're probably scared, or maybe they can't see too good. And of course you have to know that they come from a time when everything wasn't so fast like it is now, so how can you blame them, or get mad at them? But still, it's just about enough to drive you crazy, so how can you help but scream out loud in your own car?

The hardest part of the whole test was the parallel parking thing, but I'd practiced it the most, about fifty times or more, so I was smooth as a cucumber. And I smiled over at Boris, but he wasn't even looking at me. So, I dropped him back at the DMV, and before he got out of the car he told me that I'd passed, and I said "Thanks Boris, thanks a lot!" And I remember that when he got out with his clipboard and all, and started walking way, I called out "Hey Boris?" And he slowly turned around and looked at me, and I said "Thanks again, that was fun!" And he gave me a crooked little smile that made him seem not so depressed anymore, and that little moment just made my whole goddam day. It really did.

So, there I was, driving around Pasadena, going to acting school, and working as a cocktail waitress in this restaurant called Casa Mama's, a Mexican chain type of place, even though I was still only eighteen. I mean, I looked older. In fact, I'd always looked older than I really was.

I used to date a little guy back in Oregon, named Brad. I just love the name Brad. I mean when you say it out loud a couple of times, over and over, it can really crack you up. I don't know why, but it really cracks me up.

I thought he was really cool, because he drove an RX7 convertible, and we'd go to his house and take candlelight baths, so I thought I was a real grownup, you know? I mean, I was only sixteen years old for crissakes, and I'd be taking these romantic baths with a guy at least ten years older than I was. And we'd go to this TGIFs right next to the mall of course, where they'd serve me gin and tonics. I can't remember any time when they ever asked me for an ID there, I swear to God. So, my point is that no one ever questioned me about my age. I suppose that back then it was a real thrill to me, but now it makes me sad. I'm not sure why, but it does.

I'd gotten the job at the Casa Mama's when I first moved to Pasadena, and had always taken the bus to work, but it was so much nicer once I had my own car. It was the kind of place for lonely ten-story-building business type people, who got together after work for Happy Hour, while families waited for their dinner tables in a section of the bar or in the lobby, seated on these quaint Mexican style wicker bench type deals. You know, the kind of place where you deliver a lot of chips and salsa to people that only sit there for five or ten minutes or so. You waste a lot of chips and salsa in those kinds of restaurants. Once, on a very busy Friday night, I spilled an entire tray of margaritas on a little girl who was around five years old. It was pretty terrible, mainly because she was screaming and crying. I really hate it when little kids scream and cry like that. I mean, it's enough to break your goddam heart for crissakes.

I became friendly with most of the waitresses and bartenders who worked there, particularly with one of the girls named Patti. She was a half Asian girl who turned out to be the epitome of organization, as far as waitressing goes. She really taught me everything valuable about being a cocktail waitress, not only how to be friendly but not *too* friendly with the guys for that extra dollar, and how to really sell. And after I'd worked there for a while and became accepted as one of the girls, they all took me to their after work bar, which was one of those steakhouse bars with a cozy gas fireplace in the middle, that also had live music on the weekends. We used to drink shooters called Hot Shots in the winter, Kahlua and a floater of coffee to make it hot. That was our own special shooter. I'd been going there with the whole gang for about six months when the worst thing happened. I met Stu.

At the time, I thought he was one of our bartenders because of his short little crew cut. I just love rubbing crew cut heads, like I used to rub my dad's head when I was little and he was in the Army Reserves. And walking up behind him, I put my hands over his eyes and rubbed his funny little crew cut head and said "Guess who?" And when he turned around and I saw his face, I met trouble. I mean, there I was, a young woman of eighteen, not wanting to meet anyone, because I was so involved in school. And I'd been behaving myself for so long, because I hadn't really known anyone here in the city, and was really only partying a little, you know, after work and all. I was so involved with memorizing scenes, and working on my voice, and reading drama history and all, that nothing had distracted me from it, especially men.

But when he asked me to give him a ride home, and said that he had cocaine, I was completely swayed. I hadn't done any kind of drugs for almost a year, not that I'd done a lot of drugs before, maybe a little pot now and then, but not really cocaine. It was kind of exciting to me, and it was the 80s after all. I mean, everyone was doing cocaine back then. And when we got to his house in Altadena, it was so great. Well, it seemed great to me because he had so many books, and so much big beautiful furniture in this big house, with all these different bedrooms and a big old fashioned kitchen with one of those old gas stoves. And Stu seemed so together.

And that's when my world started to change.

CHAPTER
9
TRUST

After I became Stu's girlfriend, everything went downhill. I became totally obsessed with cocaine. I became the worst type of addict I could ever imagine myself to be. I finished the year at my acting school fairly well but not well enough, I am ashamed to say, because I wasn't asked back for the second year, which was something most of the students strived for. Before the cocaine, I had wanted the same thing, but once the downhill thing had started, I didn't really give a shit anymore about anything in my life at all.

I never told anyone about it, you know, about how I really felt. And, at least I didn't have to tell my parents or anything, because they were way the hell out of the goddam picture. And the fact that I'd even say that means that I really did care about what they thought. But truly, at that time in my life, I didn't even know if they cared that I was going to school in the first place.

A lot of other things went bad too. I was fired from my job at the Mexican place, because one of the waitresses had asked me to sell her an eighth, and after I sold it to her, she sold me out to the management. I mean, this chick was a trip, because all of us waitresses from the restaurant took this little vacation on a weekend together to Palm Springs.

We drove there in one car, and had a very good time along the way. And once we got closer to our hotel, I brought out the cocaine that Stu had given me for the trip, and she was perfectly willing to do it right then and there in the car. And she was the most fiendish of all, asking me for more all night long, while we were in this club, dancing and drinking.

I thought she was a perfectly fun girl, and that even though she was so much older than me, that she related to me as a person. She was this really tall black woman that had the best butt I'd ever seen, and when I wore my little Mexican style skirt I felt like a little kid next to her. We spent a lot of time talking about our lives in the club that night, so I thought I could trust her, you know? And then, there I was, sitting in the manager's office, him asking me if I'd ever used cocaine, and I said no. And then, I remember that I was very quiet because I was afraid.

He told me that this waitress, whose name I can't even remember either, like so many other people I've known in my life, had told him that she'd seen me in the bathroom taking cocaine, and that I'd offered her some, which was completely untrue. He was this really thin French man, the kind of French person you can just picture walking around in Paris, with a thin little mustache and a big beret. Of course, he never actually wore a beret, but I could easily picture him in one. And he had a really pinchy little face, like he was just mad all of the time. I kind of felt sorry for him because he never really seemed very happy.

And about the waitress, I mean, after the trip to Palm Springs, she had me bring her cocaine at least once a week. I don't know what happened. I guess she was just tired of me or something. I just walked away. I'd never been set up before. I was just trying to be a nice person to her, and was completely blackballed instead. But, I learned a great lesson from that experience. Never think anyone's your friend just because they want something from you.

I have to tell you something. Even though I know that now, it took me a lot of years to really understand it. I mean, after being raped, and having lived with a workaholic dad and a controlling mom, I should have known better. I think that should have been enough to make me not trust people. But I was still willing. I felt I had enough stamina in me to keep me going, I was still so young. And the thing that really pisses me off is that no one ever warned me. I swear to God, no one had ever told me not to trust.

Only nine months earlier, I had written this stupid poem about how much I loved all people, and how special they all were. But the only reason I thought this was true, was from this stupid little *God Moment*. You know, one of those moments when you get all clear and bright and everything seems to glow and you feel like crying because you feel so happy all over, and you feel all safe, like nothing bad can ever happen to you again. Have you ever had one of those? They're pretty great, but they don't happen too often. Well, at least to me they don't.

Anyway, I'd found this four leaf clover, so I decided to make a wish of happiness for all people. I was sitting on this really green lawn in the Pasadena heat, under a tree in a park that was right across from my acting school. Actually, that lawn was amazing to me. Most of Pasadena didn't have lawns nearly as nice as this one, because of the heat there and all. And I knew about really green lawns, coming from Oregon. It was a really green lawn. This happened right after I'd given my cashier's check to the school for my tuition. I mean, I felt like it was a God moment, and I felt like He was talking to me.

Now that I think about it, I know He was. It wasn't stupid. It was beautiful.

CHAPTER
10
THE TRIP

C ocaine had fucked me up. A year of acting school, gone. As much as I wanted to be a serious, studied actress, after taking all of these acting and singing classes, and paying one hell of a tuition, I just kind of quit, you know, just kind of gave it all up to cocaine. In my drug brain, it just seemed like a waste of time, and a waste of money. But also, when I came to LA, I had no idea that the acting business can basically use the hell out of kids from Ohio or Kansas, you know, young people with dreams of stardom, and a belief in themselves like I'd always had.

But it was a school that was pretty hard to get accepted to, and I really was proud of myself for getting in. Everyone in the acting school had voice class with this really handsome teacher who'd written this supposedly famous book called 'Your Sensuous Voice.' It was a pretty fun class. We would give neck and shoulder massages to each other to loosen up the muscles around the voice box. One of the weirdest parts of that class was *painting the walls* with your voice. I'm not sure I really understood the entire concept of this particular exercise, and I really didn't learn a whole lot in that class, other than how to give a really great massage. Of course, we also had the mean dance teacher, and the singing class, and another acting teacher whose husband was some famous guy on Cagney and Lacy. She was very passionate and would always squat down on her knees and say "OK! All the emotion you need is…*right here!*" And she'd thump on her chest and say "And all you gotta do is drawwwwww it up and….

Phooooom! It'll come right out!" And she'd be panting and squatting, and just smiling like crazy at everyone.

And then there was Francine, one of the scene study teachers. She was very interesting. She walked into the classroom every single day, wearing un-matching socks, saying through her coffee and cookie filled mouth, in her glorious Brooklyn accent "Okaaaaay, who's taking role tuhday?" Then she'd sit on her chair, munching on her coffee dipped cookies, and watch us work through our different scenes, squinting through her glasses, and only ever saying after almost every scene "That was so baaaaaaad! What are you tryin' tuh do, mooooove me? I mean, I could sit here and move that mountain over there faster than you! I mean, that was so baaaaaaad! Get off the stage. Who's next?"

But the truth is, that I actually felt pretty good in her class because all she ever said to me was "I can't hear you…get off the stage." in a very quiet voice. To me this meant I was a good actress. Actually, she and the passionate one were the only ones worth the money in a lot of ways. At least to me, they were. They both demanded excellence and truthful passion, and hated over-acting. And those were both important things for me to learn.

It was near the end of this first and only school year, that I got a call from Oregon. It was my best friend Nikki. She was one of the girls I mentioned before that I had taken care of in high school, and she said that she'd had a real bad case of spinal meningitis, and how she thought I should help her get away from Portland. She'd been hanging out with this pretty messed up woman who was also a heroin addict, and had gotten her into it. She said she'd like to come back down to LA with me if I came up and visited, and maybe I could try to help her get her shit together.

At that time, I still was not really speaking to my mom, and I hadn't spoken to my dad for a while, but I thought if I called him up for a trip there, he might take me up on it. And the place that Nikki was staying was close to where he lived, so I thought it would turn out real convenient and all. Right after my school term ended, I flew back up to Portland, and my workaholic truck and camper driving dad actually showed up on time. But he didn't smell like coffee, more like Red Label scotch, but it didn't really matter at the time. I mean, I'd had a couple of gin and tonics on the plane so who was I to judge him, you know?

And we actually did spend a pretty pleasant evening together, with dad sharing his scotch with me, and he fired up the old barbeque and made us some salmon steaks he'd caught himself from his yearly trip up north off the coast of Alaska with the guys. He seemed to always have a pretty good time on those trips and all, and was always sending me photos of them out on the boat, dressed in their fishing gear, their faces covered in several days' growth of facial hair, holding up their prize fish they'd caught. I mean, it was pretty darn adorable, all these old guys probably feeling like a bunch of teenagers, drinking their beers or whatever, farting, and telling all kinds of stories, and all that kind of guy stuff.

After we finished dinner, and put away a good deal of his Red Label, he broke out the old cribbage board, and we fifteen one'd and fifteen two'd the night away, and it was like I was an eight-year old again, for crissakes, without the scotch of course. Now that I think about it, it was about the best goddam time we'd ever spent together. It really was. Which made me feel real bad about what happened afterwards.

The next afternoon after dad had gone to work of course, Nikki and this girl Bonnie, another friend of ours who went to school with us, came over to good old dad's apartment, and we all made fun of his ugly rented furniture. It was all really bad upholstery and fake wood coffee and end tales, and it kind of made me feel sorry for him, you know? But I had blow on me, so we got the hell out of there, and went to Bonnie's apartment that she also shared with her mom.

Now, Bonnie's mom had always seemed to be the coolest parent on earth. At least, I had thought so when I was in high school. A few times after school, we'd hung out with her in their apartment and smoked pot, and she could take the bong hit of all bong hits, I swear to God. She was this tiny little squat woman that kind of reminded me of a Troll, and she actually had boyfriends, which always amazed me. I mean, she was really unattractive. But, she'd sit there and tell us all about this sex she'd had the night before, with all kinds of details that I really didn't even want to hear, but it was kind of fascinating, imagining this little Troll woman doing all of these things with men. It just didn't seem natural, you know?

And now that I think about it, she wasn't really cool at all. I mean, what kind of mom gets her own daughter addicted to pot, and talks about sex all the time. I don't know, I just think it's wrong in some way. And actually, about five years after we saw her, I heard that Bonnie killed herself. There must have been something that really bothered the hell out of her for her to do something like that. And I really think it had to do with her childhood. Maybe it was because her real father had raped her. She had been only ten years old when it happened, for crissakes.

Nikki, Bonnie and I stayed up all night, doing coke and smoking pot, trying to figure out the plan, after Nikki told me the truth. It wasn't spinal meningitis, it was her fear of becoming addicted to heroin, and she needed my help to get her away from it before it got too bad. I honestly don't know how we had the money for it, but we got her a plane ticket. And I did call my dad from the airport, after being gone all night, and me worrying that he would be worrying about where the hell I was. But he didn't sound worried, he just sounded busy, and I was high, so I really don't remember the conversation, but I think he forgave me. At least, I like to think so.

By the time we were on the plane, we were pretty sober again. Nikki didn't like flying, but I made her look into my eyes when the sun was coming straight through the window. She said she saw things in them she'd never noticed before, different colors, and long legs of orange lines winding themselves around the iris and back again, like spider webs. Every time she started to get nervous, I'd distract her by telling her stuff, you know, about my acting school teachers, or about my car, and sweaty old Boris at the DMV. I just kept distracting her until we had landed.

I know now that she was really only nervous to be away from the heroin.

CHAPTER 11

COCAINE

I hate to think about this time, only because it is truly a blur, and also because putting it down into words will probably never affect the person hearing it as it really was. But it's so much a part of the story that I know I have to try and tell it, you know what I mean?

Nikki did help in getting me away from *my* drugs, and I helped get her away from the heroin. There were, what seems to me now, only hours filled with us sitting around Stu's house, drinking whatever was in Stu's kitchen to keep the edge off of our cocaine brains, and Nikki's post-heroin mind, and practically talking about nothing, even though it felt like we had bared our souls to each other, the kind of drug talk you feel so enthralled by while it's happening that you don't even know what everything really is, or what you're really saying to one another. Of course, everyone who has done cocaine completely knows what I'm talking about.

Cocaine. It's evil. And after about two weeks of partying like this while I'm calling in sick to my new job, I am fired from yet another waitressing job, a restaurant I can't even remember the name of because of being so fucked up all the time. The truth is that I was definitely fucking up. But the reason I kept telling myself was not the truth, it was the voice of cocaine. What I kept telling myself was that I just didn't feel happy there.

There were too many white tablecloths to replace, and too many little white candles that had to be lit every evening at dusk before I got to go home to do more cocaine. But the most convincing argument I had for myself was that there were all of these older women who came in to have tea in the middle of the goddam afternoon. You know, all of these rich Pasadena women that probably didn't have anything else to do in their stupid lives, besides shopping. I bet those women did a lot of shopping in their spare time.

They called it *tea* or *lunch*, but most of the time all they were ordering were martinis, or Tom Collins, or margaritas for crissakes, and I didn't think that had anything to do with tea or lunch.

I'd say to myself that it was just too hard for me, being from Beaverton, and pretending like I even wanted to be their goddam servant, because that's how they treated me. I just couldn't do it anymore. I didn't want to serve a bunch of ugly, older women, who thought that talking about their Harvard daughter's upcoming wedding, or having to decide on what stupid fucking fabric for the curtains in the guest quarters was vitally important to the universe. I mean, the whole thing was just making me sick.

That's what I told myself anyway.

Control. What I'm really talking about is control. Control of oneself, control of emotions, control of your desires, your future, your dreams. What I'm really talking about is your future and my past, and what I've learned from it, and what I couldn't see when I was living it. Spiraling. Spiraling out of control, but still believing. Still.

I mean, there were some really sick times with Stu. Like the time when the three of us ended up in a ménage a trois, only because we were so high, and truly thought we loved each other enough for it to be all right. And maybe it was all right for them, but for me it was quite another matter altogether.

I was a part of it for a while anyway, but when Nikki and Stu started really getting into each other, I just lost it. I just tore myself away, and just stood there watching these two people I thought I loved fucking each other, and it made me crazy. Maybe I thought I was in love with both of them, and that in this act they were betraying me in some way. They were the two most important people in my life at the time, and there they were, ignoring me, completely.

So I went into the shitty little kitchen of my ugly studio apartment that only had a Murphy bed for crissakes, and decided to kill myself. And I remember I wrote this stupid letter about feeling like I was some kind of reincarnation of Marilyn Monroe, and that I was trying to get the nerve up to cut my wrists, when they finally came in and stopped me from actually going through with it. I guess they must have heard me moaning and crying and all. I mean, who knows?

Maybe if I hadn't been moaning and crying, they would've just kept going at it, and I'd be dead right now. I really don't remember a whole lot after that, but I do know that I was pretty upset. I'm sure I don't remember a whole lot because I don't really want to.

And then there was the time when Stu thought he was being set up for a big drug bust, so we had to pack up all his money and drugs, and whatever we needed for an out of town trip, and we all drove north, away from LA, and into the mountains above Santa Barbara where we found a cheap hotel for a few days, until he finally calmed down and was sure he wasn't being followed. We'd run out of cocaine by then, so we *had* to drive back. I don't know what I was thinking, or why I was so supportive and all, but he did have the drugs, and I'm pretty sure that's why Nikki and I went along for the trip.

I did run into Stu years later, and he was off the drugs and had started selling women's clothing, so that was a pretty great thing to see. I wouldn't ever wish him any harm, and I know it was just a time in our lives when we did some stupid things just because we thought it was fun.

This whole period of my life I'm about to describe is so hard to remember. I mean, I can't even remember how I was getting by, how I had the money for bills, rent, or even gas. I've tried to ignore it, but it just won't go away. And maybe that's why I have to put it down on paper. Maybe I just have to admit it so that I can forget about it. Just chalk it up for experience, like I said before.

But, you know what's so funny? You just get reminded all the time, from stuff that surrounds you, or from places where certain things happened. I mean, they just surround the hell out of you, and keep reminding you of the things that you want to forget. Like every time I see a red Mustang, or when I'm driving in Venice Beach, or Beverly Hills, or Marina Del Rey, it just brings it all back up.

It never goes away.

CHAPTER 12

VENICE

Nikki and I, finally in a sober moment, decided to get away for the day, away from Stu and his cocaine. I had known that I had to get Nikki off the stupid heroin trip, but what I'd done instead was to get her all into something else. I truly thought at the time that it would make it easier for her. But the truth is that I was making it easier for myself. I was running away from everything, not only away from Stu, but also the mistakes of my Pasadena world. I knew everything about it wasn't good for either of us. And I just wasn't paying attention anymore, I just wasn't.

Of course, we had no where we were going, or even where we should go. So we decided to go to the beach, because it was a beautiful day. In fact, Nikki hadn't even been to the beach since her arrival in LA, and it just seemed like the right thing to do to get our minds off all the crap.

You know, the ocean, the beautiful, vast, all powerful mother of all life creating ocean. It would feed us maybe, and clear our minds and inspire us. Anyway, that's how I felt. And the funny thing is that I thought we'd be safe there. But it turned out to be the most fateful, the most unsafe day of all. It was domino day, when the pieces all start to fall, boom boom boom, right in succession, slow at first and then faster and faster, and it's all started and you can't do a goddam thing about it.

Venice Beach. I knew a few things about it because I'd spent a little time around there in my early California days. It was the only beach I knew to go to, other than Playa del Rey. But Venice was completely different. People there just blended all together somehow, and left other people alone to be whatever they were. I knew they wouldn't even notice that we were pretty lost at that time in our lives, and that most of them wouldn't even really care if they did. I mean, sometimes people can see you in a place and know you're in trouble, like the people in the Mexican restaurant in downtown LA. I hate to go to Venice Beach even now, because it's not a happy place for me anymore, and I'm not sure it ever will be again.

There's every type of people you can think of there. Like the Japanese photo takers, the fat American tourist parents with their fat American tourist kids from all over the country, the sexy half-dressed Italians, or the LA city people trying to get away from the inland summer heat. But you mostly notice the homeless ones, or the drug-selling locals on their skateboards or bicycles, hustling, or the usual bad street performers. Like the guy with the big dirty white turban that plays guitar, while he sings some Eastern Indian sounding songs, and skates all up and down the boardwalk while smiling this really big fake smile, just to make tips off people. I mean, he'll skate right up in your face while you're walking along, and won't leave you alone until you tip him. It's pretty annoying.

Most of the people are just walking around like everything is fine. But when you really look at some of their faces, you can tell it's not. I don't mean that everyone there wants to slit their goddam wrists for crissakes, but you can really tell the difference between the people who are happy and the ones who are just pretending. And sometimes that's a good thing, because you can just go there and blend in, and you don't feel one way or another about who you are, or care about who you are with, and you're able to just observe the life going on around you. You know, just try to understand, and just see everyone as just innocent little children. And, sometimes, it just makes you feel better.

But when you have to spend the night there, it's completely disgusting. I mean, I never dreamed I'd have to spend the night in my own car, or that I'd ever be homeless.

We got to Venice in the late part of the morning, and drove around on Ocean Avenue, writing down the numbers of places with for rent signs out front, and then we just parked and went to the boardwalk, right at the beginning of its southernmost point. It happened to be a Saturday, right in the middle of summer, when the boardwalk is at its peak of the year, just packed with all those people I was telling you about, and we're walking along in our shorts, me with my shapely legs, and Nikki with her beautiful long dark hair and long legs.

Now, let me tell you something about Nikki. It wasn't that guys didn't look at me all the time, but for some reason Nikki was just a goddam guy magnet. I mean, she was always smiling her big, beautiful, Italian smile, and laughing a lot, and she was a real boisterous girl, always yelling something out to complete strangers, just to make them laugh, you know? She was a really fun girl back then, and I liked that about her, that she always wanted everyone around her to enjoy themselves too. I thought that was pretty special, that she always wanted to share. I liked being around her, I just did.

We were passing by the paddle tennis courts, the little, short versions of a regular tennis court, where you play with short paddles instead of the normal long handled tennis racquets. And actually, I did play once, but I kept missing the ball because I was so used to the longer version. It was pretty frustrating. So, we're just walking along, and Nikki's smiling away, and probably singing a song or something, and this really cute, curly, dark haired guy calls her over to him. And he's sweating away after his paddle tennis match or something, and wiping off his handsome dark face with a nice clean white towel, and he asks her if she'd like to go to a party with him later on. So she says yeah, and he tells us to come back to the courts around four o'clock to meet him.

The rest of the afternoon was pretty nice. We went to the Sidewalk Café, a landmark on the boardwalk, where you sit on the outdoor patio, and most people just get loaded on margaritas, and we probably shared a good burger or something, and flirted with more guys, then just walked the rest of the day away, until we ended up back at the paddle tennis courts to meet the dark-haired guy, but he wasn't there. But Buck was.

Buck was tall and lanky, with strong legs and brown wavy hair, and tan freckled skin, and very charming. You know, with one of those real reassuring faces, and his slow southern drawl seemed very kind. We asked him about the dark haired, handsome guy, and we didn't have a name, so we just kind of described him. Buck said that he had a list of phone numbers for all of the regular paddle tennis players at home, and said "Why don't y'all come over, an' I could make a few phone calls an' see if I can reach him, an' I live just down the road an' all." I mean, he seemed so gentle and reassuring, that we felt safe enough.

So we followed him there.

CHAPTER 13

BUCK

Now it's going to get really hard for me. Because I have to remember it all. I mean, I have to put it all down on paper. I hope you understand that. That it's really hard for me to do this.

I mean, I've read a lot of worse things about other people in the world. And, in fact, I've seen them, personally. There's a lot of pain out there. But now that I think about it, it just means that I'm not alone. I guess I was pretty wrong to say that we're all alone, because in the end we really are but we're not, you know what I mean? I suppose that's what gives life meaning, at least it does to me. And that's a good feeling. It really is.

So, we follow Buck to his condo in Marina Del Rey, just south of Venice Beach, following him in my beat up old red Mustang, right behind him in his brand new Jaguar XJ7 convertible, and park in his visitor's spot, while he parks in his garage, and he has us follow him upstairs.

On the beach. I mean, truly, right on the goddam beach. This glorious condominium right on beachfront property, for crissakes, with three bedrooms, and a huge balcony with all this beautiful patio furniture that you could just fall asleep on if you wanted to, just go right to sleep listening to the waves. And we're walking around, and he's showing us his place like it's nothing, you know, like he's practically a vagabond for crissakes, saying stuff like "I know it's not much, but *I* like it." I'd never been in a place like it, being from a lower to middle class family and all, if you know what I mean, so I was impressed.

He had us sit on his big white couches in the living room that also had lots of animals heads with antlers on the walls, while he got out his list of paddle tennis guys, and started making phone calls. In the meantime, he offered us a glass of wine while we waited, so of course we accepted the offer. I remember this so well. You know how sometimes things just stick in your mind? It was Lancers wine, which is a kind of bubbly, yet light red wine, like a cross between champagne and cabernet. I thought it was very classy, but now that I look back, it was just a very cheap wine with bubbles in it. I mean, I thought I was in the middle of goddam Class City, hanging out there with him.

After all the phone calls he made, he didn't happen to find the paddle tennis guy we were looking for, but it really didn't matter, because after a couple glasses of wine, we didn't really care anymore. The mixture of the feeling like you're sitting in luxury combined with the feeling of being lightly drunk can make you feel really relaxed and almost special, you know?

We all sat there talking for a couple of hours, and started really getting into the story of Buck's life, asking him questions and all about himself. At first all he really talked about was being divorced, and that he just worked all the time. He said he was an investment banker, and we said we thought that was pretty great, as if we even knew what investment banker was, for crissakes. But after more questions, he really started to open up. He said that now he was just really one of these lonely men, who had been through the whole drama of Vietnam. You know, the fear he'd felt while he was there, and the horror he'd seen, and he started crying, and just kept right on crying, and snotting and everything, while he was describing these guys who'd died right next to him. Nikki and I just sat there listening to his Vietnam War stories, and we kept bringing him tissues, and pretty much forgot about all of our own problems.

It made my life seem so trivial, just so goddam insignificant compared to his. And even Nikki, the strongest person in my life at that time, the girl who'd been through all kinds of stuff with her family for crissakes, was moved too. I could see it in her eyes while she just sat there listening, like I was, listening and watching with her big brown eyes. And listening was a pretty hard thing for Nikki. I remember we both cried, Nikki and I, while we listened to him, and he just kept on crying too, and all of a sudden we were all crying and holding on to each other, just crying our little hearts out. After a while, we all just calmed down and started to smile again.

Then Buck asked me about myself, you know, in a very sincere way, and I started to talk about my acting career, and how I was all into it, but wasn't really trying so hard anymore, and how I pretty much had no respect for it anyway, which was completely untrue, but I said it anyway. I know now that I was just trying to sound like an adult, like someone who'd been around and was already calloused by the whole Hollywood scene, like I already knew all about it. Inside I was just as driven as I'd ever been, but life and cocaine had made me feel not so desperate about it anymore.

And then, I just had to do a monologue from Joan of Arc, for crissakes. But the good thing was that I was drunk, so I really got into it. And actually it was pretty good, as far as I remember, because it made him cry. It really did. I mean, I can do a pretty goddam amazing Joan of Arc if I want to.

When I first learned the monologue in High School, I just felt like I could relate to her fear of being locked away. Away from the green, and the life of things, if you know what I mean. She had this gift of seeing Godlike things, and sometimes I feel the same way. I see a lot of things, like on the street when I'm just driving along. People, just people in their lives, sometimes really sad, or sometimes just lost with bags in their hands, or selling oranges and flowers in the middle of an intersection with enormous traffic, like the one at La Cienega and La Brea. You know, selling roses for someone else's wife, while theirs is probably cleaning somebody else's house in Beverly Hills, or struggling away trying to find Pampers at K-Mart for a bargain.

But, sometimes I worry that other people just don't understand me. Sometimes I'm just too much for people who don't want to feel. I mean if I bring up things about life and pain and all that kind of crap. They just don't want to talk about it. It can be a problem.

Buck ended up letting us stay overnight in one of the guest bedrooms. And in the morning, the maid was there, and the coffee was already made by one of those automatic coffee makers, and he'd left these big fluffy white terry cloth robes out for us, and we're all sitting out on the deck, looking out at the beach and the ocean in the morning sun, having our coffee. And out of the blue Buck says "Why don't you gals live with me for a while? I won't charge you rent or anything, and you can look for an apartment or work around here. Oh, and by the way, one of my buddie's ex-wife's an agent, so I can get you into her office for an interview, so what do you say? I like having you gals around, and we can all be friends!"

I wish I could've seen the future right then. I mean, I really goddam wish I could've.

CHAPTER 14

THE GIFT

You remember the stepfamily, the one I mentioned a while ago? Well, the thing about them is that they were witnesses of this time in my life. I guess I was pretty lucky that they were around, they were really nice people. Of course, it was never their fault, it was really just what we all thought was the best for all of us. But, I guess what I mean is if they had never been a part of my life, if I'd never left my Mom, you know, and the whole hat contest with Dad, I would have never gone through any of this. You can only make decisions about your own life by yourself, and who is to say that what I chose was not for the betterment of my life. And now I know things that I never would have if I hadn't gone through them. And after all, who actually controls one's life, right? I like to think that there is some kind of God that does, but you can never really know for sure.

And also, I suppose that Nikki, who was one of those people who might have never been a part of my life, if it hadn't been for so and so, and so on, for crissakes, was a witness too. What I'm saying is that it all really happened because of her always feeling like she was still in love with my ex-stepbrother Sean. Not that I can blame her either, yet she truly was a part of it. I didn't tell you about it before, but when I first met Nikki, I threw rocks at her.

She had come over with some friend of hers who was dating Sean at the time, and me and my stepsister Bobbi hid in one of the upstairs windows and threw rocks at them while they were sitting down by the pool, just for fun. Nikki's girlfriend pretty much fell out of the picture once Sean had gotten a good look at Nikki. It was love at first sight.

We'd been staying with Buck for a couple of weeks, and never really did go out to find another apartment. We'd wake up and be sitting around with our coffee and say that we were going to go look, but Buck would always say "Oh no, not today! I was planning to take the morning off and take you two gals to lunch!" So we'd forget all about it.

Buck was pretty funny sometimes too. Like the things he'd say about his life back in Texas, stuff about how backwards it could be. You know, stuff like how there'd be signs that said "Eat Get Gas" or "Buy One Get One". Or he'd say things like "You girls get a leg on!" He could be pretty goddam hysterically funny sometimes. And Nikki and I'd told him about how we used to exercise these horses up in Oregon on this little mountain called Mount Cooper, where we'd been so lucky to have all of these freshly carved roads where they were building a housing development, and we could let the horses just run and run on these clean dirt roads with this beautiful view of Mount Hood in the distance. And Buck would always tell us how he'd take us on a trip to his parents' ranch in Texas where we could ride in fields all day long and never see another house or human for miles. It all sounded pretty goddam romantic, well at least to me it did.

I'd gone back to the ugly studio apartment in Pasadena, and packed up all of my stuff, or at least most of it, which we stored in his garage. I was always leaving stuff behind, like the rattan chair that I thought was so cool, and my dishes that I didn't really need anymore. Sometimes it just feels good to leave stuff behind you.

One day, we were outside in the California sunshine, listening to the sound of the surf, and sitting on the gorgeous, sleepy patio furniture, when Nikki brought up her real love. She started telling Buck about her relationship with Sean, and how she missed him, and how they wished the whole family could find a way to move down to sunny California, and all. And Buck, well, he just stops and thinks for a minute, trying to act all relaxed, which is what we're used to seeing him as. But now that I think about it, he was probably petrified, and probably thinking about himself. Maybe he was in love with Nikki, I don't know. Not that I *would've* known this, or could have seen the truth, but it was there. And I couldn't see it.

And then, after a long time of silence, he said that he had a way to move them down here from Oregon, for free, and that he'd put them up in one of his apartment buildings until they got on their feet. Well, Nikki was overjoyed at the idea, and started kissing him, all over. And I felt happy for her, I really did. Of course, I still believed in Buck at that time. He'd been through the pain of life, and love, and death. He knew. I mean, I still trusted him. And he still seemed so open and relaxed, and stuff, and by that time, both Nikki and I were having sex with him. You know, intermittently having sex with him is the best way to put it. But we were definitely paying our own way by our own means.

It just kind of happened. I never expected it to, or even thought about him in a sexual way at all. Even at the beginning. The reason I say that is because he seemed so much like a missing part of my family in a way, like an uncle or something. And he wanted to take care of me, which was something I wasn't particularly familiar with, so it was kind of nice. In fact, the caring part seemed to me like a gift I'd always asked for, but no one knew how to give it to me.

Like the stuffed animal dog I'd gotten for my birthday. My sister had gotten hers first, because she'd asked for it for her birthday in January. So, I asked for one too. But the one I got wasn't right. I mean it was pink like hers, but it was not as soft, and not as cute. She'd named her dog Fred, and I'd named mine Charlie. Charlie never meant anything special to me. In fact, I couldn't stand him. He was too stiff, and his nose didn't go in when you pushed it with your finger like Fred's did. I didn't even sleep with him. I just left him on the floor, and then later in the closet, hidden under mounds of other stuff that I didn't care much about either. There was even this Norwegian dress that my Grandmother Inga had brought all the way back from a goddam trip to Norway, and it was just laying right there on the floor with Charlie. I feel kind of bad about that now, after she was all sick from cancer at a pretty young age, and to think of her going to Norway before she died and thinking enough about me to bring back a real authentic Norwegian dress, and me just leaving it on the floor like that.

The thing about Inga dying is pretty sad. I mean, she was supposed to go to the doctor, but my stupid Grandpa and Uncle took off to go hunting instead, so after that she didn't even want to go to the doctor. She just kept getting sicker and sicker up until the day she died. They said that the tumor was the size of a grapefruit. That couldn't have felt very good for poor old Inga.

And the worst thing about Fred is that I got so jealous that one day that I hid him from my sister. She kept going all around the house searching for him, and we got into a fight, and I actually tried to push her down the stairs to the basement. I can't believe I actually did that, but I did.

The only reason I'm telling you this is because it has to do with gifts. You know, the gifts you wanted but never got quite what it was that you were asking for. At that time I was just too goddam young to know what it was that I really wanted. Of course, I know now that all it might have been was some kind of soft affection. But I really am over Fred now. It just makes me sad that I tried to hurt my sister like that.

Nikki and I never talked about having sex with Buck, until one day when we were walking on the beach. She told me how guilty she felt about betraying Sean, and I remember telling her that it was okay, and that I understood, and how lucky we were to have Buck as a friend. We really thought that we were safe with him, we really did. And the thing about us having sex with him at different times became an unspoken thing, and was never brought up between us again. It didn't need to be. We knew what we were doing, and why we were doing it.

About a week after suggesting the stepfamily moving to California thing, Buck asked us if we'd like to go to dinner with him to one of his friend's house for dinner, who also owned part of a big luxury automobile business. He said that he was a *good* friend, and that he liked beautiful girls, you know beautiful girls like *us* to make dinner for. So we went. Of course, we didn't think anything of it, and it was something social to do with Buck. And we didn't even know, but this was the guy who owned the company that could do the stepfamily's move for free.

I remember at first that I felt so touched by Buck taking us there for dinner. It was supposed to be kind of a surprise for us. I mean, this was *the Guy*, and this was only a week after Nikki had mentioned the whole Sean love thing. And after a few martinis, a nice dinner, and plenty of cocaine and wine, the Guy assured us that if our friends needed to move down from Oregon, that it would be perfectly safe for his company to put the moving charges from Bekins under his name, and that he'd take care of it and all, even if they needed storage in the case that the apartment wasn't ready for them, and so on.

Remember what I told you before, that at that time I trusted people, and that I just believed for some reason, and I didn't know why but I did? Well, that night, somewhere between the fifth line of coke and the fourth bottle of Merlot, I started to get a funny feeling, like everything was going too perfectly, just too easily. And I probably don't need to tell you that doing cocaine again was not the smartest thing for me to be doing. I'd thought I had gotten away from it, and now I was just sitting around on someone else's white couches, you know, beautifully upholstered white leather couches, and taking walks on the beach at sunset, and in the morning after having my coffee, and I was putting on someone else's fluffy white robes, and life was great.

I'd changed. I wasn't really motivated about anything at all, or thinking about acting, and what was I really doing there anyway? I guess I felt like I really didn't belong there, and that it was someone else who woke up under the 800 count cotton Egyptian sheets, and a goose down comforter that probably cost as much as my goddam car.

The night was a blur, but I can tell you that what this man promised Nikki seemed like gold as far as she was concerned.

We all went back to Buck's feeling pretty good about the whole move of the stepfamily and all. Actually, it was this man's cocaine that made us feel okay. Truly, that was the mistake.

CHAPTER 15

FAVORS

The stepfamily did move down from Oregon. They did move all of their belongings with this company that this friend of Buck's was attached to, and they did put it all into storage with Bekins. But what didn't happen was that *the Guy* somehow did not sign for it, for the move or the storage. None of us knew that at the time. And Buck did not provide an apartment for them upon arrival. Which basically meant that the entire family, including one four year old niece from my stepmother's daughter Christina who'd died in a car accident, was now homeless, and without the delivery of their belongings to an address that Buck had also promised to them.

Now, what happened on the day they got here was not that bad. We ended up spending the day at the beach after a bunch of teary, excited hugs, especially between Nikki and Sean. And Buck himself apologized on the phone to them for not having the apartment available, but *it would be in a day or so*, and the Guy still promised that their belongings were safe.

What did happen that day is that Buck paid for a room for all six of us in a cheap hotel. He said he thought that we should spend some time together, you know, have us *reassure* them of his intentions. "The gals are living with me, so don't worry about a thing!" he said to my ex-stepmother on the phone. "Maybe y'all can come on by and have dinner at my house…sometime this week! How's *that* sound?"

They stayed at the hotel that night, and we stayed with them. And the next night, and then the next. Of course they were all worried about the whole thing, and who wouldn't be? Now, my ex-stepmother, as a whole, was a very smart, forceful and bold woman, and she kept demanding an actual date, which Buck was very easily vague to respond to, saying things like "Well, it hasn't been cleaned yet, but I *think* they'll be cleaning it tomorrow..." as if he didn't know anything. I think he really did mean to get to it, but it just never seemed to be a day closer, and the days just kept passing, like Groundhog Day.

I remember that I felt like someone looking in, and that I really didn't know what to expect, or how I should feel about the whole thing. I didn't even know what I wanted for myself. I guess I was basically a person who at that point just didn't feel anything in those particular days. But at least I was trying to help other people, so I guess that's something.

I don't want to say it, and I don't want to have to explain it, but I barely remember the days that followed, like they were a dream that you just can't put your finger on. The apartment promised by Buck never materialized, and right in the middle of it all, Buck died.

All I really remember of that time is Nikki, Sean and I being invited to the house of the Guy. I know that we were doing a lot of cocaine that night, and late in the evening, Sean and I started making out. Of course, Sean didn't do drugs at all, as far as I knew, and he was really calm and gentle, and didn't seem to mind being around us when we were high.

I don't remember how or why it happened, but it was most likely the drugs of course. Nikki came in at some point and was freaking out, of course, but we somehow calmed her down, and Sean left to go back to the hotel. Then the entire madness started. Nikki and I were left with the Guy, the cocaine Guy who offers free services all the time, while all along he is lying. He knew just enough of what to say to us that would make us believe that he would keep his promises to us and the family, but what he wanted as payment for the favors was to watch Nikki and I fuck each other.

CHAPTER 16

HEART SEIZURE

This is for you. This is just about sharing the experience, and also just to make you laugh with me.

Imagine what it feels like to see a man, an only halfway attractive man, who is wealthy enough to burn one hundred dollar bills in your face, especially when he knows you're poor, over and over, waiting to see what you would do with your closest friend, and him seeing how far he can push you, and all you can do is keep doing lines, and looking at each other, and laughing for hours about actually kissing each other, until it's so late in the morning, that you start feeling crazy, and you stop doing his lines and drinking his wine, and you tell the guy to go fuck himself, and you'll pay the money all by yourself thank you very much to get your ex-stepfamily's stuff out of goddam Bekins if it kills you. And you call for a taxi, and out of desperation you grab a handful of the hundred dollar bills he's about to burn and run for the taxi that's just arrived…

Now you're on your way home, you think, to Buck's beautiful condo on the fucking goddam beautiful ocean, but just about halfway there, your best friend starts having a heart seizure, and you try giving her CPR, but it's not working, and all the while you're screaming at the taxi driver to DRIVE DRIVE, and she's turning blue, and her tongue is rolling back into her throat, and you reach in and pull it out because she's gagging on it, and she's purple now and shaking like mad, and her spit is dripping out in long strings, and her tongue is in your fingers, but now she's white, she's got oxygen again somehow, and still shaking so hard so you try to hold her still and grab her head, holding onto her tongue again, forcing her lips apart, and then you try to push more breath into her lungs from yours, because she's starting to turn blue again, and after that you try pushing harder on her chest again with your palms, one two three, and she's still not better, she's still blue, and you're still screaming to the driver DRIVE DRIVE TO EMERGENCY, and you give her your breath some more, and push on her chest some more, one two three, harder than before, and you're breathing into her again, your lips on hers, and it seems like forever, and she's blue and then white and her body is shaking like crazy and she's drooling all over herself and you don't know what you are saying, but the driver goes on, and she's breathing again, and you don't know why but she is, and you end up in an emergency room at 5:00 in the morning, and the driver goes in and you go in, screaming for help...

And they take her on a stretcher, and you tell them she has no insurance, and they say, well we can't take her in she's going to have to go to County...

And it's all slow motion, and your friend seems like she'll die, and they put her into an ambulance, and she seems okay now, and you've saved her somehow, and you get into the front seat, and you don't even remember paying the taxi driver, and the ambulance driver is driving...

And the time goes so slow, and you ask them to drive faster, but they won't listen to you, they won't even put on the siren, drive faster please...

But they won't, and you sit in the ambulance the whole way down to Torrance, and finally they pull into a hospital after so much traffic and they wouldn't drive faster no matter how many times you said it, or how hard you cried, they wouldn't drive faster...

And after that, they just dropped us off, and drove away, and she had to walk in, for crissakes. I had her lean on me, and I walked her in with her arm around my shoulders, because she was so weak. I kept screaming for someone to help us, but no one did. In fact, they completely ignored us. Someone finally told us that they only take dying people seriously, like she had to be bleeding profusely in order for them to pay attention. So, I just sat her down, and went from counter to counter, until I got to the right one and they gave me some forms to fill out, and told me to wait.

There were so many other poor people ahead of us. The whole time I thought she was going to die, but she kept hanging in there, smiling a weak little Nikki smile. After a couple of hours, someone did eventually come to take her away. All I could do was sit outside on the curb, smoking and crying.

I must have cried for hours, and people kept passing by me. Some would even ask if I needed help, but I couldn't really answer because I was crying and shaking all over. My head felt huge from crying so hard, and I couldn't even answer anyone. I just looked right through them.

I remember that I only sat there not speaking, not seeing anything, for those hours because I felt so guilty. I felt guilty about her love for Sean and how I'd been kissing him only a few hours earlier, and for bringing the ex-stepfamily down on the promises of others. I felt guilty about taking her away from her life in Oregon, which was a pretty stupid thing, because she would have died much sooner if I hadn't gotten her away from the heroin.

My head was a balloon, and it wanted to float away. But my stupid goddam body kept holding it there, attached to the earth, and I couldn't escape.

CHAPTER 17

PROSTITUTION

How I came to prostitution, to actually prostituting myself. I don't know. I really don't want to think about it. It's just this thing that happened to me. It happened because I needed to survive.

Ignoring the instincts that I'd had at that first dinner was not a smart thing, for one. I mean, Buck *was* the kind man we thought he was, but the Guy was not. And then Buck just had to die at the wrong time. Therefore, we were thoroughly fucked in every way. We weren't lucky.

And the day that Nikki had her heart seizure was quite the wrong day to have it. Not that you can control the timing of something like that. But really, it was the worst timing possible, because when we returned home to rest after the whole ordeal at the emergency room, was the moment when we found out that Buck was gone, and we were locked out.

There was this little Asian woman standing outside his building with her yappy little black pug, just tugging the hell out of its little rhinestone leash, while she told us in broken English that Buck had shot himself, and that all the neighbors had heard it. "Oh, sooooo roouud…you can hea all da way tru de wars. My war is light next to heeees! Oh, I soooo sced! He die!"

The best thing is that Nikki didn't die. It turned out that her heart just couldn't take that amount of cocaine, a perfectly normal thing that could happen to anyone, and they told her to lay off, or the next time she probably would die.

I don't remember if it was morning, afternoon, or night. But I remember not understanding what was happening. He was gone and there was nothing we could do or anyone we could call to try to even get our stuff. At least I'd left some of our clothes in the car.

If only he had been alive to let us in, his calm face and smile would have made us feel better. And he would have known that our hands were cold with no mittens on, and that we were only five years old, out in the snow, in the cold, begging to just sit on those couches in the fluffy terry cloth robes, begging for hot chocolate and pie. But what we'd really do is drink his wine and make him feel not so bad anymore about the goddam Vietnam War. And we would have ridden the horses across the Texas fields, into the sunset.

But that didn't happen either.

To me, even today, it was one of the most frightening times of my entire life.

But *someone* had my entire life in their hands. I remember thinking this. Right then. And I was all theirs. But I didn't know who in fact had it. I thought I was an adult, that I'd been through enough to take care of everyone, and that everything was my responsibility. People would cry, and I would respond. People would complain, and I would try to explain a way to try and make it better. I'd try, and they'd believe me. They all just believed me.

I have to explain something. You see, when I was a kid I took care of a lot of things. Not that I don't know that most of you feel the same way. I'm sure you do.

I'd always taken care of myself, and knew I was self-sufficient from the beginning, you know, letting myself into the house by myself, all alone, when I was only in the first grade. Everyone else was still in school or at work at that hour. I mean, what did I need anyone else for, except to buy the food and lock the door at night. I did laundry, folded it and put it on the beds. I took care of the dog when I got home from school. I helped dad paint the house, high on a ladder, worked in the garden, knew when the daffodils would bloom on the west side of the house. I knew things, I paid attention. I was just a little kid.

My ex-stepbrother Sean had started boxing in Oregon, long before the move down to LA. So his main intention upon arriving, was to go to Punch and Judy's Gym, famous in Venice Beach, where we all ended up staying. He went there to work out, and met the owner, a female boxer named Judy, and they became friendly. So, after being locked out of Buck's, and the ex-stepfamily having to keep paying for hotels, we were all pretty relieved when Judy invited us to stay in her one-bedroom apartment for however long it took us to find a place.

This meant a one bedroom apartment with six extra people in it, and Judy also had an occasional roommate, Gail. And considering the understandable frustration my ex-stepmother had toward me at the time, I tried not to spend much time there, unless I really needed a shower, or to sleep somewhere other than in my car.

Judy was a very intense, thin, blonde, breast implanted, early thirties gal that looked nothing like the character in Punch and Judy. I'm sure that she appreciated Sean the way most women did, which was probably the reason she'd let us all come to her apartment in the first place. In fact, Sean flirted with her, *not* with Nikki, which I'm sure made her a tiny bit upset from time to time, but we were all so saturated by the madness of it all, that no one really cared what was happening.

To say the least, we really didn't have much fun together. And my poor little step niece still smiled for all of us. Just to have someone who was still innocent kept us all from killing each other.

I was out trying to find a job in yet another restaurant in Venice when I met this girl who called herself Jamboree. She was this beautiful, really short and thin black girl from New Orleans. She told me that she was being kept by a very wealthy Japanese man, and that I could make some extra cash by going to see a friend of his, this man who liked being touched by a lot of girls all at once. At first, I just laughed, but I remember seeing the seriousness in her face, and her saying "You'll get a hundred bucks."

It was my first time getting paid. I don't remember a lot about that night, other than stroking his penis and seeing him come on his stomach. That's all we did, and it didn't seem so bad.

After that night, I'm not sure when exactly, but most likely within the next couple of days, I met up with Jamboree again for a coffee or something, and started telling her the whole story about how I felt so responsible for the predicament I'd put these people in, and she told me she had the perfect person for me to meet.

Jamboree said to let the whole family know that she was taking me to a friend of hers to work in what she said was 'marketing', and that they should start looking for a place to call their very own. I was going to be making lots of money.

Soon.

CHAPTER 18

MEETING THE MAN

Jamboree met me outside Judy's apartment, and we only had to drive a few miles to get to the house of The Man. He also lived in Venice, and to this day I know exactly where that house is. I've driven by it hundreds of times over the years, but have never had the heart or strength to ring the bell to see if he's still there. Or bring a gun to kill him just in case he still is. Soon after this time in my life spent with him, I really thought I could kill him. But time passes, and life hopefully teaches you to think better of things, and you choose to leave those thoughts alone.

I never learned his last name, and I'm very happy to this day that I never did. He was just The Man. Maybe he was a very thin, dark skinned Vietnamese midget, or maybe he was a fat little English guy. But I won't tell you that here, and it really doesn't matter what he looked like or what his name was anyway. He was a very well-spoken man, very gentle in most of his ways.

At the age of nineteen, I was definitely lacking in knowledge regarding the world of prostitution. Not that I should have had any previous knowledge, or had ever given the subject any thought whatsoever. Money was something you worked for, did labor for, that was what I was used to.

But when I met The Man, and because of the way he spoke to me, I felt a kind of wishing that I understood the things he said, as if his type of education had something to do with a higher level of worldliness. Just the idea of the world of him still makes me nervous.

I had no idea what he was saying to me, or why. In fact, while writing this, I have no feeling other than that of wanting to throw up. What he constantly talked to me about was the money I was about to make, how much better off I would be, how I could send my family away in smiles, and how I would also prosper in the future with my young body. The young body I had. That's what he talked to me about, in his dark living room, while I just kept getting more and more coked out, with nice jazz music playing in the background, him telling me in his quiet voice that I should be proud of who I was, that the way I spoke was classic, that I was a pretty thing, and after all of the cocaine he gave me, I just sat there and listened, and even at three in the morning, he chose that I should stay there with him, him talking to me alone. And then he sent Jamboree home, who I'd even forgotten was there with us. But of course, not in the same room. I'd been all alone with him for hours. He made me feel special.

I want to tell you about one of the last times I worked for The Man. I truly thought that it would be my last.

Not that I actually had a career in prostitution. I didn't. I really only did it a few times, less than fifteen or so. And only one guy actually wanted intercourse, with a condom of course, but he was a pretty nice guy, and took me to the racetrack to bet on horses, and he was very kind and very appreciative, and fun to be around. In fact, I wondered why he wanted a prostitute at all, but some guys are just like that, they want to have sex with strangers, and just leave it at that.

With what little experience I did have, in that short time, I learned that you'd never be subjected to men having to actually *like* you. I mean, it seemed like you could just go to an *appointment*, and that nothing would ever hurt you, and that nothing they ever said would be important to you, that the feeling of giving to someone else would just be natural. Being natural was always something I expected from myself, but couldn't achieve once someone was an asshole. And once they were an asshole, I couldn't behave. I just couldn't be nice or natural for them, because I felt loathing for them with such a passion that there was no way to just be myself. And that's why I left.

The one time I left was so great. The last time. Well, almost the last time.

So. It was this guy. He was full of money, and he was full of himself. He was a really ugly, bald, short, and kind out of shape guy, a little doughy. But of course, I'm just trying to describe him as he was, right? He had me meet him downtown LA at the Bonaventure Hotel, which used to be this pretty cool, upscale high-rise hotel with a revolving restaurant way at the top of the building. It's usually a romantic place for a dinner date, you know, an anniversary, or a proposal or something like that.

Anyhow, I met him upstairs by the elevators like he said, and we were escorted to our table, and I said thank you after he'd pulled out my chair and all, all proper, and all I can remember after that was that he said things like "Well, you're going to *fuck* me, right?" Maybe it was the way he said *fuck*, all strong F or something, like it was something horrible. I don't know, he was just really nasty and very degrading, saying things like "Oh, you think I'm going to let you order for yourself? I know you want something *expensive*, but you know this is *my* money here, so don't order anything too *expensive*, you hear me?" Things like that.

I remember thinking that I'd just order a slice of lettuce with a side of one olive please, or something ridiculous like that so that the waiter would know what an asshole he was. And then I remember we were eating, and I heard him say something shitty to me again, so I excused myself to the powder room, trying to sound all proper, and I left the table. I had planned it. The whole time sitting there not listening to him, I'd been planning it all in my head.

I took the elevator down. My heart was beating so hard, and I went down and I found my car in the parking lot, and I had this, I owned this, my first car, it was all mine, and I'd paid for it, and I got into it and I drove away from the Bonaventure Hotel. I remember the freedom, driving towards where I lived, and how great it was, to just be getting away from the fucking asshole. And that was almost the end of my bad times.

But it wasn't.

The next morning. Not knowing where I was. Not knowing why I was there. And then, The Man, wearing a robe in colorful red, gold and brown, making me coffee and eggs. Me, so hung over and starving, and not knowing anything. Now I remember where I am. I'm still staying at The Man's, and I'm hungover from celebrating my escape from the asshole from last night. Only sipping the overly strong coffee, and seeing the Venice sun outside the windows, and glad to be away from Judy's.

At Judy's my ex-Stepmother would be waiting to hear about my new job, all supportive, and Nikki would be sulking and ignoring Sean and being mad at me for not telling her where I had been, the niece either crying or running around wildly wishing for, demanding to go to the beach, or Bobbi, poor Bobbi probably trying to find a job herself and pretending that everything was okay.

And while drinking my coffee that morning, I imagined myself calling Marie on the phone, saying *He talked me into it. He talked his way into my mind to be a prostitute. It's all right because I'll give you all the money anyway.* Then in some beautifully emphatic and compassionate way, I would remind her how people had always talked their way into our lives, like when she was young and her guard was down, and she got married. *Remember what you told me, Marie? We're better than this.* However, the conversation never took place. The Man kept me there, or at least persuaded me that I *should* be there. And super high on coke, again, I actually drove my car to Judy's to get the few things I still owned. Not that driving while high on cocaine is the hardest thing to do, not like driving drunk and seeing double. It's just intense.

I still had a key, and was amazed that it still worked for some reason. Luckily, no one was there, and I remember I knew that that was a very good thing. I just took it all and disappeared back to The Man's sanctuary. He always made me feel like I was doing a good thing.

Nikki left soon after all of this. I'm pretty sure I can't remember why because I was so high all of the time. She went back to South Carolina, to her grandmother's house. I was glad to have her gone. One less person to worry about, after the whole heart thing and all. Even though I thought of her as my best friend, I hoped someone would take better care of her than I could. I even drove her to the Greyhound bus station and everything, and after some tearful goodbyes, she said she'd keep in touch, but I didn't think she would. I never thought that. I think I even gave her the money for her bus ticket.

And now that she was gone, I could concentrate on something better for myself for a change. Drugs.

Like I said before, one of the things I still think about is the nightmare of the moth. But it wasn't actually a nightmare at all. That's just what I call it because I still have dreams about it. I mean, it just *felt* like it was a nightmare. I was two years old, and in my crib, and I remember waking up when this enormous moth flew into my face. At least it seemed enormous to me. And then I was standing up and leaning on the railing, crying.

I remember that I was crying for someone to help me, but no one came. It kept fluttering and fluttering, its wings buzzing around in my crib, and against the glass of the window to the outside light. You know, that horrible sound that moth's wings make when they're fluttering around a light bulb inside a lamp.

Well, anyway, the thing about it is that no one came. But I still have dreams about it.

I even had a dream about it the night that Nikki left.

CHAPTER 19

INDEPENDENCE

Now I was truly alone. I gave the ex-stepfamily some money, and left them for good to fend for themselves. I was able to put a little money into a new bank account, to save for a future move, because staying at The Man's was not such a happy thing for me anymore. He sent me on a few easy jobs where all I had to do was sit or stand around for guys who wanted to jerk off while I played with myself. I mean, it wasn't that bad, and it wasn't like I had to touch them or anything. Plus, it was really good money.

But the men were really unattractive, and my heart started getting to me, because I would feel all nauseous and shaky whenever I had to go to a stranger's place. I remember I always had to take a bath afterwards, not because any of them had touched me, but because it somehow made me feel better.

But, I really had to get away from The Man. One night, in the middle of the night, I woke up to one of his other woman friend's dark brown pussy in my face. She was older, with white skin and hard eyes, and thick, dark, wiry hair, and straddling me and staring at me passionately, saying things I can't remember, and was obviously a cocaine addict. Skinny, with hard breasts and she rubbed and kissed mine fiercely and roughly, and The Man sat in his chair in the corner, stroking his cock, and he talked to me, saying "Touch her, make her come." I didn't know what to do, so I let her lick me and pretended to come, while she made herself with her own fingers, while biting my nipples. I faked it, and I was good. And the only goddam reason I knew it was because the next day The Man said I could move out. I could quit and go. I had pleased him. The Man, staring at me with his dark eyes, like a snake.

That very morning, I remember going to this little outdoor patio breakfast place in Venice that was very popular in those days, and had some eggs or an omelet or something, all by myself and feeling free again, but now in a very different way. The best thing was that I hadn't done any coke for a few days, so my mind was clear and I knew I was done with it. I just didn't want it anymore. I think that leaving the asshole at the Bonaventure had awakened some kind of new strength in me somehow. And sitting near my table was this pretty nice looking German type man eating breakfast with his friends, and he noticed me.

His name was Yan, and we got to talking. I told him I'd just moved here from Oregon, as The Man had instructed me. "Leave no trail." he'd said. And this Yan guy told me he had a room for rent in his house in Venice for $300 a month, just a few blocks away, which was also his father's house. So right after breakfast, I followed him there to take a look. It was a nice, small, older house with a big front yard, and best of all, a private bathroom with yet another claw foot bathtub, just like the one I'd had in Pasadena.

I remember at the time, I felt as if it was a new beginning. My troubles were over, I had some savings, and I was about to get a job, or at least look for one seriously. And I still had my car, and now a real place to actually live. Of course, I had to lie to him, and say that I just had to go back to my friend's place where I was staying, and get the rest of my things, you know, just to make sure he didn't know my true situation, that I wasn't really living anywhere. I think that he kind of knew in a way, but I left and drove around for an hour, and then came back, and brought my suitcase and the rest of my stuff into the house.

The rest of my stuff. What a joke. I'd only managed to keep one of the ugly green plastic suitcases and one small box of books and my radio. Everything else was long gone, but the only thing I really missed was this really ugly green crocheted frog with arms and legs that were all about 3 feet long. I used to tie it around my neck, or on top of my head to go get groceries, you know, just to make people laugh. It was a pretty funny looking frog.

The bedroom itself I remember clearly. I don't know why, but I do. It had darkish green walls with dark wood molding, and high ceilings, and wood doors, I mean, real wood doors, heavy and private, and it had big lightly curtained windows with sunshades on three sides looking out to the garden, which Yan Senior, Yan's father, looked after. And he did a beautiful job, I can tell you. I mean, the grass was so green and level, and there were beautiful shady California trees, and so many roses. I'd never seen so many rosebushes, except the ones up in Oregon in the Portland Rose Garden in Washington Park. He even said I could cut roses for my room if I wanted to. And I did. I'd open all the windows to let in the fresh smells from the garden, and the air from the ocean that came all the way to the house, even though it was fifteen blocks away. It was always clean air, always breezy there, and the sounds of the trees rustling was a beautiful thing.

The house was quiet, and smelled like a hint of cooking and also the smell of men. It kind of reminded me of the way my Norwegian grandparent's house up in Washington State, way up in the mountains, but I think that must have been just the smell of Old Spice and old people mixed together, kind of disgusting if you really think about it, but I guess it was just kind of comforting or something. I bought groceries and put them into the fridge we would share. I remember buying healthy things, from this small market called Mother Gooch's, vegetables and fruits, peanut butter, and good bread. And the nicest thing of all, I thought, was that Yan put a radio in my room. I didn't have the heart to tell him that I already had my own radio.

The day after I moved in, I went to this very busy restaurant in Marina del Rey called Carlos and Pepe's to find a job, any job, even working in the kitchen if they needed me. Of course, on the application I had to lie about being fired from my previous jobs in Pasadena, and could still give my old references up in Oregon. At least I had an address to put down, which was a real good thing. Sitting there at the bar, waiting for an interview with the manager, there was a group of older men, sitting around watching football and drinking beers. Of course they asked me what I was doing there, and told them I was trying to get a job, and one of them asked if I had any experience in accounting. I remember I said that I didn't, but that if I had a chance I knew I'd be pretty damn good at it, and they all laughed. And do you know what? The guy actually took me up on it. He told me to meet him at his office on Monday and 8:30, so of course I said yes, and left right away. I didn't even wait for the manager of Carlos and Pepe's to come out and interview me. I just left, feeling more confident than I had in a very long time.

Now, I think when I look back, that what I did that morning, the morning I met Yan, had to do with the feeling of a new life. A chance to start over. And that's what I was trying to do, just start over, and believe in myself again, a newborn baby, all fresh and free, and someone who'd had no problems. Just erase them, just forget. But the thing is that I was still the same person, all afraid and full of fear like any other natural person, just trying to hide again in the midst of the city. And I was still me.

Now, at first, I was pretty happy to have someone believe in my natural talents, and as a matter of fact, I thought my new boss did. I went to work on the Monday he told me to come. His office was in this very large penthouse condominium, where he also lived, and did all of his stock trading and business accounting and all. I proceeded to organize everything he'd been working on for the last five years, the years where he'd tried to do it all himself without a secretary. And I just did the natural thing that I thought anyone would do, you know, alphabetize, file-by-type, minimize, arrange by months, years, calculate write-offs, and I swear to God, I was great at it. Not just good, I was great. And it only took me a couple of weeks or so. I don't remember what he was paying me, but I did know that it felt a whole lot better than being a stupid waitress.

I mean, I didn't have to be charming or funny, or even interested. I just had to be quiet, and work steadily. And, I have to say, his papers were truly in a bad state of disarray, but I fixed them, and straightened them into a system any child could understand. I truly did.

And then one day, he asked if I wanted to go on a little trip with him and his friends, up to Lake Arrowhead I think it was, for a little fishing trip. We drove up there in his beautiful Mercedes, all smelling that kind of leather smell only a Mercedes has, if you know what I mean. I swear to God, they all smell that way. So we meet his friends and go fishing in the warm sunshine, but of course they all bring a lot of booze on the boat, and then we go home to the beautiful little woodsy house surrounded by all these big pine and fir trees that reminded me of Oregon. It was just all woodsy and peaceful, and we all pitched in cooking their freshly caught fish dinner, and of course we're all drinking tons of vodka and grapefruit juice, and listening to the old guy's music, you know, Glen Campbell, and Johnny Cash, and Patsy Cline, and they're all singing along, and I'm trying to sing along, but I don't really know all the words, but we had a pretty good time, singing like mad out on the balcony, under the bright stars that you can't see if you're in a city, and just breathing in the scent of all the dark trees surrounding us.

But then, I wake up in the morning, and I'm only wearing my grey sweater, and sleeping next to me is my boss. I mean, this old man, who was probably almost seventy years old for crissakes, and it just grossed me out. I mean, he was a nice enough guy and all, but he was mostly balding and grey. We didn't have sex, because I 'd have known if we had. But the worst thing was that I'd wet the bed and I just felt ashamed, and had to shower right away. And then I had to strip the bed and try to hide the wet sheets, but all I could do was leave them on the railing of the deck outside the room to dry.

I remember feeling real funny while we all sat around drinking coffee together, because of the way the other old guys looked at me, and the way they smiled at my boss. That's when I remembered how they had laughed in the bar when he'd asked me if I knew how to do accounting. But nothing had happened at all, except for me wetting the bed. Of course he probably didn't tell them that, but it made me feel a little uncomfortable if you know what I mean.

The whole drive home to L.A. was very quiet. We hardly spoke, except for him talking about what his plans were for future trading, and me just saying yeahs and uhhuhs the whole way back, just because I was just so goddam embarrassed. And he just left me in the parking lot, waiting for my Mustang from the valet guys, because I'd met him there before the trip.

And he didn't even pay for my parking bill, even though he'd said he would. It cost me three days of working for him. He was old, and he probably just forgot.

I don't remember a lot about the job after that, but I think I was paying his bills and keeping his accounts straight, but I didn't feel like there was a whole lot for me to do. I do remember that he had the financial news on the television 24-7, and that I'd never even watched the stock market before this, and found the whole thing to be very frustrating because I just couldn't grasp the concept of it, no matter how many times he tried to explain it to me. I guess he wasn't a very good teacher. And then one day, soon after the trip, he told me I could have a week off.

I remember I was glad, because we never talked about what had happened on the trip, and I was really glad he never brought it up. I still planned on coming back to work for him, to learn more, to learn to be a really great secretary like my mom had been. I still had faith in the skills I believed I was learning, nonetheless.

CHAPTER
20
BUSTED

I was worried about money. Of course, I said nothing to him about this when I left the office, but I felt it all of the time.

I still had some money in the bank, and had paid my rent, so I was still somewhat safe. On the evening I came home from work, I'd bought some wine for myself, and tried to head straight for my beautiful green room, but had to go into the kitchen to borrow the wine opener. Yan noticed I seemed a little sad, and asked if I was all right, and asked me to eat dinner with them, but I went to hide in my room instead.

I wanted a puppy. I don't know why I wanted something else to take care of, but I did. I asked Yan the very next day, and he looked at me in this kind of despairing way, as if he knew that his father disapproved of me, but still he said yes. I don't know why his father didn't like me, but maybe it's because I was young, and wore really short shorts quite a bit. But he never really talked to me, and pretty much left the room whenever I was around. And maybe he didn't like that his son liked to be around me a lot. I will never be able to explain what was there between us, but it seemed like some kind of understanding between misfits, the kind of loneliness that only people who feel the same thing in themselves can understand, even though they've always thought it was their very own individual and completely unique feeling. But there it is, completely visible in some stranger's eyes, like a mirror image of what's in your own. I don't know. That's just the only way I know how to explain it.

I went to the local animal shelter in Culver City, and found a tiny female German Shepherd puppy that a woman had left there because she couldn't feed her. So I paid the fees and took her home and named her Joe. I'd always wanted to name a dog Joe, boy or girl. She was so thin and light, but I bought good dog food to fatten her up.

The next day, she kept throwing up, and I was really worried, so I took her to the nearest veterinary clinic, so close to the house that I walked there with her in my arms. They examined her and said she just had typical kennel flu, and gave me antibiotic drops, and said to keep her in and give her the medicine twice a day for the next week. And I had to spend more money for her, but I was willing to keep her alive. I really was.

And I did. I kept her close, and rubbed her soft fur and belly, soft and promising. Yan kept wanting to come in to help he said, but I just stayed alone and turned on the radio. Morning came, and she seemed a little stronger, but I started worrying about money for food and gas, and food for Joe. I tried calling my boss, but got no answer.

Later in the morning, Yan brought the phone to my door, a call for me he said, and only a couple people know I'm here, and it's him. The Man. "How are you?" he asked. I told him about my new job and the new puppy, and I was really nervous for some reason. And he says he has a job for me, more money than I've ever seen before. And I try to tell him I'm done with it, I don't ever want to do it again, but he says "Listen…are you listening? *Fifteen hundred, two hours.*" he says. And rent is due in two weeks, and I'm almost broke, and why hasn't my boss answered my phone calls, and how am I going to get into acting, all of this in a flash, and I'm scared.

"Okay." I said. *Okay.*

"Meet me at my house, Thursday at five, I'll drive you there. Bye sweetness." Dial tone, and I just sat there listening.

Thursday. Wearing the light green dress with the embroidered collar that Nikki gave me as a present, kind of bohemian, but sexy. I could tell you that I was feeling bad about my choice, but I wasn't. I mean, fifteen hundred cash, and maybe more if they asked. But I was nervous, sweating a little like I always did before an appointment, wondering what they would want for that kind of money. And The Man saying "Sweet one, just drinkers, partners from out of town. Don't worry, big cash for *nothing* as usual."

Marina del Rey. The International Hotel. The café. Four men there in a booth. The Man left. Three other girls came and sat with us, along with a scary woman with rings on her fingers and bells on her ankles, saying "You kids go on and have fun now, we'll see ya layta!" And walking away alone on silver tipped stilettos, she instantly vanished from the café. Through the windows we could see her cross the parking lot and get into a very expensive looking Porsche, looking very rich.

The four men got up and told us to follow them. We crossed the busy street to this big six story hotel, tripping across the street dividers until it was safe to pass. It felt like we girls imagined the men needed to stop in the lobby for the room keys, but they're telling us they've already got them, come along with us, and so we do. Then they split us up, two for two, and the next thing I know, I'm walking away with the bigger of the two guys and the raunchiest of the three girls, and I'm thinking "Oh, God! Not *her*!"

We enter the room, and the guys go to the fridge, and are saying things like "Hey what do you girls want, a soda or something?" and the raunchy pro says "I don't want anything but *champagne* and a *cock* in my mouth!" just cackling away like some morbid witch. And the two guys laugh, and one of them says "Yeah, we'll get you girls some champagne, but first we want to know if you girls will go all night or not?"

Now this didn't shut up the other girl at all. I mean, she was all over the place saying "Yeah baby, whatever you boys want I can give it to you, but for a *price*, ya know, like at least five grand…" and I'm kind of saying "Well…no, I don't know…I don't really want to do that…"

And the next thing you know the handcuffs are on us, and they're practically *dragging* us out of the room, along with the other two handcuffed girls and two men, and we're all put into these unmarked police cars, and we're all driving away, into oblivion. Just sailing away into oblivion.

On the way to wherever, the big undercover guy tells me that he will be kind to me, you know, in his report about me. But he's not. Of course, I wouldn't know that until I'm in court two months later.

In his report, I later find that he has lied and said that I was the most prominent of the women in the rooms. And you know what? He smiled the ugliest smile I've ever seen to this day, on his way out of the police station where they dropped us off. But for some reason I still believed he'd be good to me with his report to the judge. Even then, I didn't know what that kind of smile meant.

I'd never seen that smile before in my life.

There I was, in jail, wearing my green dress with the beautiful embroidery on the edges. I was in a kind of shock. It was a big room, with a semi-wall divider that had worn painted benches on every perimeter, except for near the caged window where the female guards pass through all of the stuff for us. And, for some reason, I remember it being a bad minty green paint on the concrete block walls, and bad fluorescent lights. I only say this because I don't remember a lot of the details of the entire time, but I remember what it looked like. But not the people, never the people. Believe me, I've tried to remember them, but I can't.

And even though all the walls had those benches, there still wasn't room for everyone to sit. I had gotten there early, in the early evening, but no one made me move when it became crowded with women later on.

I was completely surrounded by all these women from other places, places like South Central, East LA, Riverside. I don't know where else, but it doesn't really matter. I kept feeling like they would kill me. I'm one of two white women in the Sybil Brand prison hold, which was one of the harshest women's jails in LA County, I now know. Through the cage window, the guards pushed big, worn, stainless steel trays of sandwiches made with white bread, butter and wafer thin ham, which the dominant ones passed out to women they liked. For some reason, I turned out to be one of the ones they liked. Maybe it was because I was quiet. Expressionless. And I didn't talk. Or cry, like a few of them did, or complain, loud and ugly. I just sat on the bench. So when the sandwich passing, or more important, the cigarette passing times came around, I didn't rush up to the passer like all the others, I'd just meander up behind the crowd and ask nothing, say nothing, except for my outstretched hand, complacent.

Easy. Easy, I kept thinking to myself, easy will do it. And it worked. The huge black woman who was the main one in control somehow liked it that I didn't beg. At least, that's how it seemed to me, because everyone else who was yammering and threatening around me, and demanding things from her was ignored.

But I just stood there like a stupid person that just didn't care, like those starving children you see in those TV ads where they just stare at the camera with no feeling at all. They have nothing to say either. I'm not sure why this instinct came to me so naturally. Maybe it had something to do with my childhood that taught me survival. Just let them fight, and don't say anything. And then one day, you'll be gone and won't have to hear it anymore, and everything will be so much better.

My one and only phone call, of course, was to The Man. I didn't believe him when he said he'd come and bail me out and drive me to get my car, but he did. He really did. He picked me up in a car I didn't recognize. We barely spoke the whole way, but now that I think of it, I was probably sleeping, which was something I'd barely done for the past three days.

I do remember something that happened while we were driving though. There was a car that almost swerved into us while we were on the freeway, and my body got this white hot flash. That's why I tell people now that I think I'm going to die in a car. It's the whiteness of it, the deep gut feeling of a short instant of pain, and then, nothing. It still happens to me all the time.

We pulled up near his house, and my car was actually still there. I don't know why I thought something could've happened to it, but I guess I was just worried about one more thing going wrong. And then I was gone, away from him again. No pimp fee for him, I thought, no reason to talk. Thanks. I think now, that I actually thanked him. But of course I would have. No decent girl from Beaverton wouldn't at least say thanks for a free ride somewhere.

CHAPTER 21

THE PAPER

The minute I started walking up Yan's driveway, his father started running down the lawn from working on his beautiful rosebushes, wearing gloves and carrying clippers, saying "You're not staying here anymore, you're *not* staying! *Tramp*! *Whore*!" He was shaking his gloved fist with one hand, and brandishing the clippers at me like I was some kind of hardened criminal, and it just made me feel awful, and I was all sick inside. It just made it all worse with his words and screaming and his little gloves and all, and looking so much like a grandpa that I'd wanted to make proud of me someday.

He must've heard me parking my car on the street somehow. The poor old man was shaking and yelling so loud that I was worried about him. Yan came to take his old father away, trying to be gentle. He said that what had happened was in the papers, and that I'd have to move immediately, his father was not well, and the neighbors all knew. It was on the front page of this local free rag, and all of them knew I was involved.

Of course, I was in a pretty numb state of mind, but I went into the house to get my stuff, and then I remembered Joe. I realized I hadn't even really thought about her much. I mean I'd *thought* about her, but I just imagined she'd be fine, and that Yan would take care of her. I mean, I was more worried about my car for some stupid reason. But she was gone. I couldn't find Yan anywhere to ask about her once I'd gotten to my room, so I just ran out of the house and through the streets, calling and calling for her, but got no answer. Only neighbors looking at me funny, and talking amongst themselves. I knew then that Yan had given my puppy away.

I'm sure I was mad. I'm sure that if I'd had the courage I would have sought Yan out and asked him about it. But I was broken, truly broken, the kind of numb where you just want to sit down and cry and scream and howl, but you just can't, you just have to keep moving and breathing and thinking that something will make everything okay again.

I even managed to call my old Boss. But, he said that he'd seen the paper too. I mean, it was a local paper, so whatever happened there was known by everyone in the area, and he said he couldn't help me. He was even angry with me for letting him introduce me to important people who worked with him. I just kept saying how sorry I was, and that I was scared and needed my money, so he told me I could come get my final paycheck from the valet guys downstairs.

I got off the phone feeling like a different person. I could go away from all of these people where no one knew anything about me.

My last phone call before I packed up was to the Fat Man. I only call him that because I can't remember his name and it's nowhere to be found in my diaries. I'd met him through The Man of course, and had only seen him once, but for some reason he'd said to call him if I was ever in trouble, so I did. I guess it's good that I don't remember his name to say it out loud here, only because he was so kind to me. He owned a fairly prominent business on Wilshire Boulevard in Beverly Hills. And the one time I had met with him before, he only wanted a blow job. We had gone to his back office and he sat in this huge black leather puffy chair, and leaned back. He probably weighed at least 350 pounds, had a very large face and very black hair.

So after picking up my last paycheck, the last money that I knew was mine, that I'd actually earned, I drove to Beverly Hills.

———∞◦◦⦿◦◦∞———

The place I met him was this horrible little hotel on Crescent Drive, a street just on the edge of the best places in Beverly Hills, and only 3 short blocks from Rodeo Drive. It was a small kind of hotel, only 2 stories, and maybe 20 rooms. It was probably real cute and charming when it was first built, the early Spanish style with old deco lamps on the lobby walls, and a big wood reception desk and very dark green walls. I mean, it must have been pretty goddam beautiful back in the heyday of early Hollywood, the kind of place where Marilyn Monroe had stayed when she first came to town. But now it was old and seedy, the very essence of seediness. The carpet was worn and the receptionist couldn't have cared less who I was or why I was there with a very large Italian man in the middle of the afternoon, looking all scraggy and un-showered in my stupid green dress that hadn't been washed in almost a week.

The nicest thing that happened that day was that the Fat Man didn't even want anything back. He left me to myself, after paying for a week in the hotel, and giving me some cash for food and stuff. He said he needed to get back to work, but I'm sure he just knew somehow that I really needed to be alone, but he did say that he would check in on me. As I said before, he was kind. The truth is that I would even see him in his convertible Bentley driving around Beverly Hills with the top down, with whom I imagined was his wife and kids, and all of them smiling and talking amongst themselves. I mean, I knew I could have yelled out his name and gotten him in a lot of trouble. But you wouldn't do that to someone who helped you. Would you?

I imagine now that the minute that lady who had set us all up, just went skipping on out of the restaurant after leaving us girls with the undercover guys, must have met with some fate of some kind herself. At least I hope so. I never read the paper, so I'm not sure what it said. What I am sure of is that her name was in there, because mine sure as hell was. Of course, this was back in the days when Google didn't exist, or at least I don't think that it did. I keep meaning to go to the paper in Marina del Rey and look at their archives, but I still haven't done that yet.

Maybe someday I will.

CHAPTER 22

HOTEL ROOM

May 10th. The room, how to describe the room. Most important is the smell. I could never figure out where the smell came from. When I smelled the sink, it didn't seem to come from there, or the shower, or the toilet. But there it was, consistently there, permeating all things. Acrid. Evil. Persistent.

It was eggy, sulfurous, and the funny thing is that I never did anything about it. No candles, no incense. I think it was because I was just so goddam grateful that I had a roof over my head, and I didn't want to make any waves or draw any attention to myself in any way.

It was a 2nd story room, about halfway down the narrow upper hall with more very worn carpet, on the north side of the building, with I guess about 10 rooms on each floor. The funny thing is that I don't really remember seeing other people in the hotel other than the guy that I'll tell you about later, and of course the occasional receptionist. And I really didn't hear other sounds, other than a typewriter, intermittently tapping away somewhere near the end of the hall. I felt like a ghost sometimes, like I was all alone in a big building, sleeping, thinking, smoking, and wondering what the hell to do with myself.

There was a small shower room with a toilet, and the sink was in the main room, with a closet, a dresser and a bed, and one window that looked out at the building directly across from mine with maybe 8 to 10 feet between them. The shades of the window directly across from mine were always down, so at least I felt kind of private. And there was no way with the smell that I could ever close the window for crissakes, so I just left it open all the time. The bed had this horribly dreary faded salmon colored bedspread that was all rough with little bumps all over it. I mostly just pulled it back and sat on the sheets instead, but it sure as hell would have been nice to at least have a nice bedspread, or at least a different color. I mean, color can have a lot to do with your state of mind and all, but the salmon color just depressed the hell out of me. I know right now that if I'd had lots of money to throw around, I would have just gone out and bought myself a goddam new bedspread, or a quilt. I love quilts. They remind me of Grandmas and the country and being all happy and safe inside on a rocking chair next to a blazing fire, while the rain is just pouring straight down outside, or it's snowing or something.

I still had my clock radio, so at least I had music. And at least the room had a phone, so I called my dad, and left a message on his machine with my address, and asked him if he could help me out again, and that I really needed just a little money to get my own place and that I'd had some troubles and all. I thought he would help me out, I really did. And the thought of that made me kind of relax a little, so I went out to get something to eat because I was starving and finally realized that all I'd had for a couple days was those stupid ham sandwiches at Sybil Brand. I mean, I was starving.

I walked down Crescent Heights Drive to this building that had lots of offices on the second floor, and other small stores on the bottom floor, but the best place was this Italian restaurant, that also had lots of outdoor seating, small tables with white tablecloths under umbrellas, and lots of Italian and Persian looking guys, just sitting around drinking cognacs and espressos and talking non-stop, I mean yelling practically, but I guessed that that was just the way they talked. And of course they noticed me, glancing at me, and looking away, and looking back again. But it didn't seem as if they'd bother me, so that made me feel comfortable. I probably had some pasta and of course a café au lait, and lots of water, because the water was so bad in my room, and then I walked over to Thrifty, which was only half a block from the hotel, and bought some wine and cigarettes and went home to sleep.

I do remember that it was pretty hot, so I just slept under the sheets, after drinking most of the wine and smoking like a fiend. At least I was smart enough to buy the wine with the screw off top, because of course I didn't have even a goddam wine opener to my name. I didn't even own a glass or a cup, so I just had to drink straight out of the bottle.

I spent the next day like that, going out for Italian lunch, coffee and water, and then to my room to think, and write in my diary and drink wine, and just think. I was really depressed and just didn't know what the hell to do. And one of the worst things is that the parking lot where my Mustang was parked kept giving me parking tickets because I just didn't keep track of the time, and just didn't want my car too far away from me. I guess I thought that I wouldn't be there for long, and that I'd just pay the tickets later.

Then, on the morning of the third day, there she was, the crazy old lady from the room with the window directly across from mine. It was kind of scary at first, because she was just screaming at me, but now I just laugh about it. She stood there with her very old, extremely sagging old lady breasts right in front of the window, completely naked, and I couldn't see her face because it was hidden by the blinds. But she was screaming at me "I can walk around naked too! I have boobs, I have *boobs*!" She just kept screaming away at me. I think I just stood there too stunned to say anything and just stared at her, until I finally snapped out of it and shut my blinds. And all throughout the next few days, I'd hear her muttering slightly, although the only word I could distinctly hear was boobs.

The worst thing is that I had to keep the blinds shut, and it was hotter than ever, and the smell was really starting to get to me, and I just kept getting more and more depressed. I'd even gotten to the point where I just laid on the corner of the bed so I could try to get some fresh air by the window where she couldn't see me, just all curled up like a little child. And of course by that time, I hardly went out of the room at all. I just stocked up on wine and cigarettes and pretzels, and smoked and drank myself to sleep for what seemed like weeks, but was really only a few days. And then it was my birthday.

When I woke up there was a letter under my door. Or a card rather, from my aunt Ruth who lived in New York. Now, I haven't even mentioned my aunt Ruth and there's a reason why. She was the one who had yelled at me the most when I had wanted to leave my mother to be with my father, and we hadn't even spoken since then. So I really didn't feel like I needed to mention her until now. Anyway, it was a goddam birthday card in which she'd written *"How dare you bother your dad asking for money. Take care, and Happy Birthday."* I mean, what the hell is that, and how was that just supposed to make my goddam birthday any better for crissakes? I thought it was pretty crappy to tell you the truth. I mean, I should have saved the goddam card and shoved in her face all these years later. But I didn't. I just threw it away. Of course, now I know she was just being protective of my dad, and she'd taken the time to send me a card and all, but it made me sad. It really did.

I'd spent the last four days in this room, not speaking to anyone, and I felt like I just couldn't take it anymore, I just had to get away from the smell of the room. Luckily I had half a bottle of wine left, so I drank that for breakfast and decided to go for a walk, because the wine had obviously made me feel a little better. Since I hadn't even ventured anywhere around Beverly Hills I decided to head on over to Rodeo Drive, you know, do some window shopping and cheer myself up a little for my stupid birthday.

But once I got there it was just terrible and didn't help my spirits at all. I mean, there were just too many pretty people, and men in suits and ties, and rich women, and pretty cars, and very expensive restaurants and shops. It was just like that scene in Pretty Woman, where Julia Roberts just feels horrible and everyone keeps looking at her funny, and she has all this money to spend and no one will help her, or anything. But of course, I didn't have the money she'd had. To this day, I love to watch that movie because I understand all about it. I really do.

Driving In LA

So I decided that that was it. I went to Thrifty and bought a huge bottle of vodka and some sleeping pills. I just couldn't take it anymore. I mean, I was just so sad, and lost and I felt like nothing could ever get better again. I had a good place to do it, and so I just sat on the bed and started drinking. The radio helped a lot, and I just sat, and smoked and drank, staring at the sleeping pills and listening to music and depressing news about the really bad LA water quality.

A couple of times I passed out, and woke up again, and drank some more, and just passed out again. Finally, somewhere around dusk, I'd woken up again, and just said *"Fuck it!"* I literally said out loud *Fuck it*, the first words I'd spoken in days other than ordering lunch at the Italian place for crissakes. And I just downed the whole bottle of pills, and chugged a lot of vodka and then just sat there crying and crying. And finally, finally I fell to sleep.

I guess the good thing is that I'd had too much vodka, so somewhere around midnight, I woke up and started for the toilet, where I threw up all of the vodka and most likely all of the pills I'd taken. I had to crouch there by the toilet for quite a while, but I managed to crawl back to the ugly salmon covered bedspread on the floor by the bed and fall asleep again.

I woke up to a sunny blue sky outside my window and the birds were just chirping like hell, and the typewriter tap-tapping away again. What I really wanted was some coffee and of course some aspirin, but that meant I needed to go out again. I brushed my teeth and got my purse. The typewriter stopped its tapping and the birds stopped chirping. And when I opened my door, there was the man from the typewriter room limping right towards me, and I kind of said *"Oh"* in a small little voice. But he just kind of slowly passed by me in that narrow little hall, and called out back behind him, just barely turning his head, he said "It's gonna be a better day." And he just kept limping along down to the end of the hall and down the stairs until I couldn't see him anymore.

I didn't know if he had been speaking to me or to himself. But then it just hit me, and I smiled for the first time in a long time. I locked my door, and went down the hallway, and down the stairs and out the front door of the hotel.

And stepping out into the sunshine, there I was.

"Each of us has lived through some devastation, some loneliness, some weather superstorm. When we look at each other we must say, I understand how you feel because I have been there myself. We must support each other because each of us is more alike than we are unalike."

Maya Angelou 2012

Author's Note

Many names, descriptions, locations, and circumstances have been altered in order to protect some person's identities.

About the Author

Brenda Bakke has been a professional actress since 1985, starring in numerous films and television series. Her release of this novel has been an undertaking that has spanned over 20 years. She was discouraged by many in the industry, who told her that some parts of her story, although told from another character's voice, could be a deterrent from being hired in Hollywood. But as Brenda likes to say "Everybody poops." She hopes her story will bring you some laughs and some encouragement, but most of all that it may help you remember to always be proud of your past.